L. RON HUBBARD

IMAGES OF A
LIFETIME
A PHOTOGRAPHIC BIOGRAPHY

L. RON

LIFE

IMAG

A PHOTOGRAP

HUBBARD

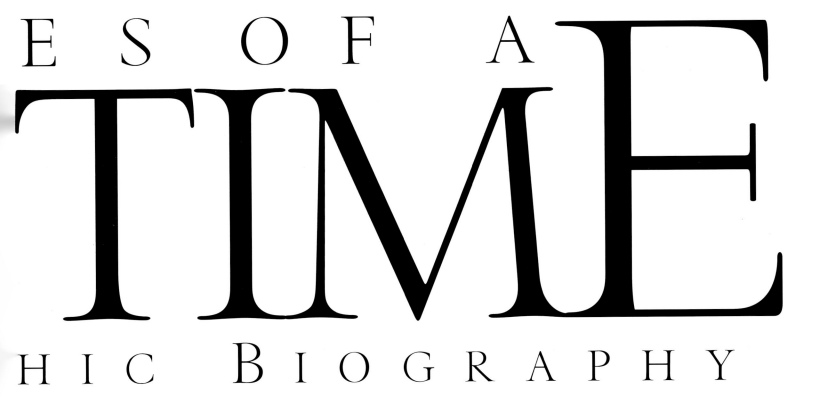

ES OF A
TIME
HIC BIOGRAPHY

Bridge Publications, Inc.
4751 Fountain Avenue
Los Angeles, California 90029

ISBN 1-57318-028-9

Photograph page 85 (top), Mark Wanamaker;
page 154 (bottom), American Stock Photography.

Printed in the United States of America

"To know life you've got to be part of life, you must get down there and *look*, you must get into the nooks and crannies of existence, and you must rub elbows with all kinds and types of men before you can finally establish what man is."

L. Ron Hubbard

C O N

Photograph by L. Ron Hubbard.

TENTS

INTRODUCTION

For all that has been said about L. Ron Hubbard—as the founder of Dianetics and Scientology, as an internationally acclaimed author, as a world renowned humanitarian, educator, adventurer and explorer—nothing speaks of the man in quite the same way as the photographs presented here. By the age of three, he tells us, "I knew exactly where I was going," and one need only examine his early portraits to grasp the truth of that remark—the gaze steady and determined with a certainty well beyond his years. Similarly he tells us, "My life has been full of strong environmental contrasts," and even a cursory glance at the pages to follow will bear that fact out: a boy in a rough-and-tumble American West; a youth in an elegant and mysterious East; an author about town in Manhattan; a leader of expeditions across three seas; a researcher and lecturer in cities across four continents. Finally, and very simply, he tells us that he never intended to make a story of his life, but only wished to understand his fellow man, to help men understand themselves and otherwise serve as at least one friend in an often lonely world—all of which seems perfectly clear when we look into his eyes.

For those unfamiliar with the larger events of L. Ron Hubbard's life, the broad strokes are these: Born in 1911 in Tilden, Nebraska, his early years were spent in a typically Wild West Montana with periodic jaunts to California, Oregon and Washington. As the son of a United States naval officer, however, he was soon sailing for rather more exotic lands, including then remote South Pacific ports and a prerevolutionary China. In all, he logged more than a quarter of a million miles before the age of nineteen and was otherwise well on the path of his greater life's journey by 1929. Thereafter, and regardless of circumstances—university, the conducting of a mineralogical expedition, the launching of a literary career—he never once wavered from the track of research ultimately culminating in Dianetics and Scientology. With the founding of those subjects in 1950 and 1952 respectively, he became the man in the bulk of photographs here: author of the all-time best-selling, self-help book; Executive Director of the only major religion born in the twentieth century; provider of solutions to civilization's most crippling problems, and source of a route to spiritual freedom embraced by millions worldwide. Also presented here are the lesser known aspects of the man as a remarkably accomplished musician, filmmaker, master mariner and a magnificent photographer in his own right.

As a final introductory word, mention should be made of the altogether herculean effort behind this work, the literally thousands of hours spent collecting and cataloging photographs from the many remote lands where Ron's journey took him. Then, too, let us not forget that L. Ron Hubbard lived at least a dozen lives in the space of seventy years, and so even a single image from his lifetime tends to say more than any one book can tell.

THE FAR WEST

Among the first images of his lifetime, Ron tells of insufferably warm days in Durant, Oklahoma where his grandfather Lafayette Waterbury had established a horse ranch, and where he himself spent his first two years after moving from his birthplace in Nebraska. Grandfather Lafe he described as a "big, bluff man, hail fellow well met, friend to all the world." Lafe's wife, by contrast, was small, pleasant and the product of a finishing school where she mastered embroidery and the art of preserving fruit. Between them came a son and six daughters, including Ron's mother, Ledora May. While to complete the immediate family, and although temporarily elsewhere with the United States Navy, was Ron's father, Harry Ross Hubbard.

Upon the return of Harry Ross, the Hubbard/Waterbury clan pulled up stakes for Kalispell, Montana—where Lafe acquired another several dozen acres for the breeding of blooded mustangs and Harry accepted a position with a local newspaper (having previously served as press officer for the Great White Fleet). Among the notable images, then, comes a three-and-a-half-year-old Ron astride a range bronc named Nancy Hanks, and a first encounter with Blackfeet braves. It was also at Kalispell that a remarkably young Ron learned to read, rope, shoot, and ride that Nancy Hanks like the wind "with a single snaffle bit, no quirt, no spurs and a cut down McClellan cavalry saddle, the skirts of which had to be amputated so as to get the doghouse stirrups high enough for me to reach them."

When later speaking of his first real home, however, Ron would invariably cite a more civilized property known as "Old Brick." It stood at the corner of Fifth Street and Beatty in the Montana State capital of Helena, and periodically served the entire extended clan, including maternal grandparents, their son and six daughters, Harry Ross and a feisty bull terrier named Liberty Bill. Otherwise, or at least through the warmer months, young Ron and his parents established themselves on a rough tract of land described as the "Old Homestead." Situated six miles beyond Helena's limits, it lay amidst thirty-five varieties of grass and a stone's throw from dwindling Blackfoot encampments where, as those familiar with Ron's life will recall, he befriended a solitary medicine man by the name of Old Tom and received that very rare status of Blood Brother.

Yet even the lesser known adventures were fairly extraordinary, including a near-death brush with maddened coyotes, the regular braving of forty-below blizzards, the vanquishing of neighborhood bullies and a perilous journey across Rocky Mountain trails in an old Model-T Ford. These same years also saw repeated treks to Washington and California, where Harry Ross served again with the Navy, and a 1924 voyage through the Panama Canal. But in either case, and as both photographs and Ron himself suggest, he hailed from an immense country that "swallows men up rather easily, hence they have to live bigger than life to survive."

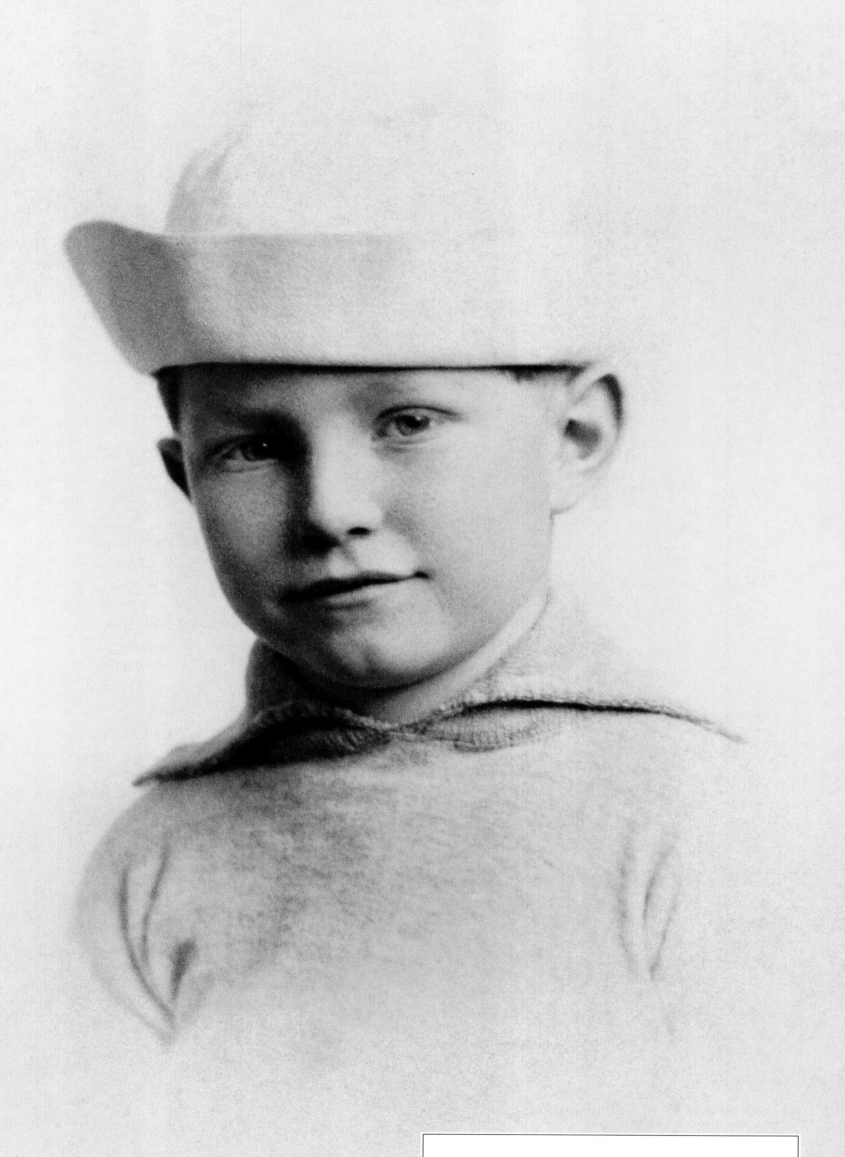

Helena, Montana; circa 1914:
Ron's parents entitled this early portrait "The Old Scout."

Ron with Grandmother Waterbury 6 months after a move from his birthplace in Nebraska.

Tilden, Nebraska; circa 1905: The Waterbury home with Ron's mother standing on porch, far left.

Ron and Mother, with Grandfather Waterbury's feed and granary in background.

Durant, Oklahoma; February 29, 1912: Ron on his grandfather's horse ranch.

Near Portland, Oregon;
circa 1918:
Ron with maternal
great-grandfather.

Among other "larger than life"
figures from a youth in
Montana, was the Blackfoot
medicine man, "Old Tom,"
who eventually bestowed upon
Ron that very rare status of
Blood Brother.

Circa 1920: Fishing with Dad while en route to Oakland, California from Helena.

Helena, Montana; circa 1917: Ron behind Grandfather Waterbury's house, affectionately known as "Old Brick."

San Diego, California;
circa September 1919:
Where Ron's father
served when not at sea
and the family resided
for just under a year.

California; circa May 1921: At the wheel of the family's Model T.

San Diego, California; September 1919: Ron and Ledora May (middle) aboard USS Aroostook on "Family Day."

Oakland, California; circa 1920: With Liberty Bill.

San Diego, California; circa 1919.

Balboa Park, San Diego, California; circa 1919.

*Pacific Northwest Coast;
circa 1920:
Where Ron and family moved
yet again following his father's
transfer to another vessel.*

Helena, Montana; 1921: A heartfelt farewell to Liberty Bill before moving on to Seattle.

Oakland, California; circa 1920:
While Father was away at sea and
where Ron attended Grant School.
"School after school. Dozens of schools,"
he wrote of these days.

San Diego, California; circa 1919: With his first camera, a Kodak Junior.

Lake Helena, Montana; circa 1921: Ron, with a friend.

Nevada; July 1920: A trip from Helena, Montana en route to California with, "Dad carefully abstaining from water when the car broke down in a limitless Nevada desert."

Santa Monica, California; circa 1922: On the beach at "Waikiki."

Tacoma, Washington;
September 1922:
First day of school.

Tacoma; 1922:
With Aunt Marnie Roberts.

Washington State;
1923.

Chesapeake and Ohio Canal, Washington, DC; circa 1923: Ron, far left above.

Washington State; circa 1924: Photograph by L. Ron Hubbard.

Washington, DC; circa 1924: Outside the National Museum of Art.

"My childhood memories consist of being insufferably hot in a swing in an Oklahoma yard . . . of watching bluebirds from a tent at the 'Old Homestead' . . . of having lots of fistfights with kids in Helena . . . of Dad carefully abstaining from water when the car broke down in a limitless Nevada desert, of rain at night in San Diego, of my uncle Bob's coffee store in Tacoma, of the awful abysses below the curling mountain roads of the Rockies, of, in short, many cities, many countrysides . . . And all this before I was ten."

L. Ron Hubbard

USS Oklahoma, *Seattle; 1923: From an early age, Ron regularly visited the ships upon which his father served.*

San Diego, California; 1922:
Lt. Harry Ross Hubbard with son.

YOUNGEST EAGLE SCOUT

O f all the various information which became important to me," Ron later explained, "such as photography, wood lore, signaling and many other subjects, the basis of it was laid in Scouting." Founded in 1910 by Robert Baden-Powell after noting the failings of British recruits, American Scouting was very much in its prime when Ron first donned the kerchief, khakis and Montana peak hat in 1923 with Tacoma, Washington's Troop 31 Black Eagle Patrol. In addition to traditional skills of backwoods survival and forest lore, he was soon earning merit badges for firemanship, carpentry, waterfront safety and navigation. Nor were these badges handed out casually. To qualify for a Physical Development Badge, for example, Ron tells of building upper body strength until he could perform over fifty chin-ups and a variety of gymnastic feats for an incorrigibly stubborn physician: "Saturday after Saturday I went back to him. He would make me chin myself half a hundred times, and then smile jovially and tell me that I wasn't good enough as yet." With the same determination, the spring of 1923 found him literally helping elderly women across busy intersections, binding injured paws of dogs, coaching a fellow Scout through the Tenderfoot requirements, practicing his bugle in the evenings, and otherwise having an excellent time.

Nevertheless, he writes, "Probably the most I ever learned was in the Boy Scouts in Washington, DC," where he landed in late 1923, with Harry's posting at the Department of the Navy. If severance from his Black Eagle Patrol had been painful, he could not have been more content with his new Troop 10, and would particularly extend his appreciation to "a great many government civil servants . . . who taught them carefully on merit badge work." But such sentiments were in hindsight, and after a truly grueling test for his Personal Health Badge, he may not have felt so complimentary. Likewise, he offers portraits of himself tramping through hill and dale to qualify for his Forestry Badge, or wearily examining stuffed finches and sparrows in a laborious effort to earn a Bird Watching Badge. Then followed the ordeal of the Lifesaving Badge in near-freezing water and many a more test of courage and skill before uncompromising examiners.

Persistence, however, paid off and, by the spring of 1924, Ron had not only earned an impressive twenty-one badges, but had led his Troop 10 to victory in the *Washington Post* sponsored Scout Advancement Competition. In recognition (only about 150,000 merit badges were awarded among some one million Scouts in 1924) Ron next served as one of four Washington youths to represent Scouting at the Presidential Celebration of National Boy's Week. It was no inconsiderable honor, particularly in light of Calvin Coolidge's very keen interest in Scouting. Yet the real acknowledgment of the season came exactly five days later when, two weeks after his thirteenth birthday, L. Ron Hubbard was named the nation's youngest Eagle Scout. It was an accomplishment not soon forgotten. (After all, only some three thousand boys achieved their Eagle Scout status that year.) Moreover, and precisely as Baden-Powell had intended, he later cited nothing less than training received in Scouting as having seen him safely through the Second World War.

Seattle, Washington; 1923:
Portrait of a Scout on the verge of an illustrious trail.

The Cascades, Washington; 1923:
Clearing trails with a local conservation corps.

Seattle, Washington; 1923:
"Visualize me in a natty Scout suit, my red hair
tumbling out from under my hat,
doing my good turn daily."

The Cascades, Washington; 1923:
With a band of hikers. LRH, first row on the far right.

Tacoma, Washington;
April 23, 1923:
"The Tenderfoot."

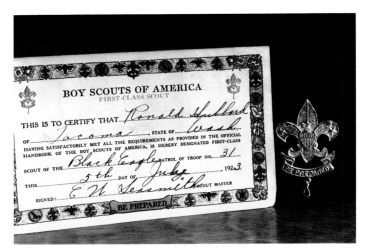

First Class Scout Certificate.

Virginia; 1924: Ron (above, far right) earning a Cooking Merit Badge.

Washington, DC; November 1923:
At Library of Congress where, quite
apart from his progress as a Scout,
Ron conducted early research relating
to the human condition.

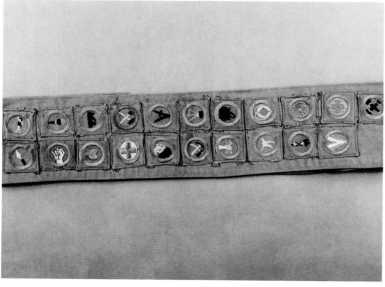

Ron's sash of twenty-one Boy Scout merit
badges earned over a seventy-five day period
in early 1924.

Montana; 1924: The nation's youngest Eagle Scout with one of the first roll-film cameras.

Bremerton, Washington;
1924:
Reveille on Puget Sound.

Helena, Montana; 1924:
The Eagle Scout medal affixed to his left breast pocket.

The Olympic Mountains,
Washington; 1924:
Photograph by
L. Ron Hubbard.

The Olympic Mountains,
Washington; 1924:
Photograph by
L. Ron Hubbard.

Seattle, Washington; 1924: En route to Camp
Parsons where he would serve as troop leader.

34

Camp Parsons, Washington; Summer 1924:
Rowing on Puget Sound.
Photograph by L. Ron Hubbard.

Camp Parsons, Washington; 1924:
Ron's prize-winning tent.
Photograph by L. Ron Hubbard.

Camp Parsons, Washington; 1924: A Scoutmaster.
Photograph by L. Ron Hubbard.

Camp Parsons, Washington; 1924:
Photograph by L. Ron Hubbard.

"OF ALL THE VARIOUS INFORMATION WHICH BECAME IMPORTANT TO ME, SUCH AS PHOTOGRAPHY, WOOD LORE, SIGNALING AND MANY OTHER SUBJECTS, THE BASIS OF IT WAS LAID IN SCOUTING. I AM VERY INDEBTED TO A GREAT MANY, VERY FINE MEN WHO GAVE THEIR TIME AND ATTENTION TO A RESTLESS, BOISTEROUS AND EXTREMELY ACTIVE BOY AND TEENAGER, AND I MUST HAVE TRIED THEIR PATIENCE MANY TIMES BUT I NEVER HEARD OF IT FROM THEM."

L. RON HUBBARD

Mount Vernon, Virginia; 1924:
A gathering of Troop 10 at George Washington's home and grave site.

Montana; 1924:
Self-portrait at day's end.

THE FAR EAST

When eventually asked what he learned in Asia, Ron would significantly reply, "I learned enough to know that man did not know everything there was to know about life."

The first voyage commenced in 1927, aboard a steam-turbine *President Madison* departing from San Francisco's Embarcadero. His course was a roundabout one through China and Japan to Guam's Agana harbor where Harry served with the Asiatic Fleet. The second, commencing a year later, returned him to Guam aboard the *USS Henderson* and then to the China coast aboard a working schooner dubbed the *Marianna Maru*. Initial notes were breezy. Notwithstanding rough seas to Hawaii, his colors remained "flying through pitch and roll," while he marveled at a fire room, "so hot the plates were red and the oil fire white." A relatively unspoiled Honolulu also proved enthralling, while initial impressions of Japan left him similarly intrigued—if slightly wary what with a "frenzy of modernization," and ominous destroyers in Yokohama Bay. Impressions from the China coast, however, were another matter entirely.

To a very real extent, the China of the 1920s was still a medieval China. For all the Communists professed in the way of reform, much of the nation still lay under the sway of the warlords—among them the seven-foot Chang Tsung-ch'ang with his harem of fifty women and legendary appetite for Western feasts. Nor had slavery, foot-binding or opium consumption been abolished; and as Ron soon discovered, an aching blanket of poverty covered all. Descriptions are dark and mesmerizing, with references to kneeling prisoners awaiting the ax, coolie songs like death chants and the knowing glances of yellow-robed monks.

Upon his return to the China mainland in 1928, the view was just as occasionally grim. By the same token, however, it was also through this second China venture that he made his way quite far into Manchuria's Western hills—to break bread with Mongolian bandits, share campfires with Siberian shamans and befriend the last of the royal magicians from the court of Kublai Khan. Then, too, as all those familiar with Ron's life will recall, he became one of the first Occidentals after Marco Polo to gain entrance into forbidden Tibetan lamaseries and otherwise drank deep from what he aptly termed "the airy spiralings and dread mysteries."

An entirely different tone marks Ron's passage through Guam—a sense of not merely moving east again, but moving into yet another wholly alien realm. Officially described as "an unorganized territory of small extent," Guam essentially served as a United States naval refueling station as of 1927. Those originally peopling the island, the Chamorros, were of Indonesian stock, and are believed to have landed by outrigger in successive migratory waves. By way of initial impressions, he told of seemingly haunted lagoons, and a forest "which is a deep green in a contrast to the sky and sea. Though it is not hard to penetrate, a thousand mysteries seem to surround it."

Here, too, adventures were many, illuminating and altogether extraordinary. He ventured into cliff-side caves to disabuse local villagers of an especially terrible ghost. He signed on as an English instructor in a native school, and inevitably ran afoul of local governors for teaching beyond prescribed curricula. He hacked new roads through jungles with a Filipino crew and unraveled native legends in a graveyard. Moreover, and perhaps even more to the point of the pages to follow, he additionally honed photographic skills to a genuinely professional standard.

San Diego; 1927:
Asia-bound with "two handkerchiefs, two suits,
one pair shoes . . . one toothbrush, two pair
socks and two pennies."

USS Henderson *at San Diego where Ron stepped aboard for his second voyage east.*

Guam; 1928: *Ron helped engineer a road along this southeast strip of the island.*

USS Henderson *at the Pacific Steamship Company dock:*
"I learned that the Henderson was leaving for Guam on the first of July . . . China or bust—now had a very sinister aspect."

Guam; 1928:
One of a dozen island studies taken (and developed) while employed at Guam's "The Photo Shop." The LRH handwritten note: "Nipa huts front the shore and the cooling trades."

Guam; 1928:
A snapshot Ron jocularly
labeled "riddle—find me."

Guam; 1928: Indigenous caribou ridden by natives in shallow
water when fishing. Photograph by L. Ron Hubbard.

Guam; circa 1928:
With Harry Ross.

Guam; 1928: "Timber hewn from an Ifil tree," reads Ron's note of this shot.

Hong Kong dockyard;
1927:
"Such a racket unloading
ship. Two coolies can
balance five hundred
pounds on a bamboo pole
and trot off singing."

Buddhist monks of
Peking; circa 1928:
Through a friendship
with the last of the royal
magicians, Ron gained
entrance to many an
otherwise sacrosanct
world.

Foothills of the Himalayas; circa 1928: An extraordinary landscape as Ron saw it on his long trail to India.

Japan; 1927: Kabuki Dancers.
Photograph by L. Ron Hubbard.

Temple of one thousand Buddhas, Peking; circa 1928: "Oh, rituals of Zen Buddhism and talking about the possibilities of this or that in hereafters and nirvanas . . . This was all quite common and ordinary to me."

The Great Wall of China; circa 1928: "I found a place one time, by scrambling over God knows how many hills, where I could get seven turns of the Great Wall of China."

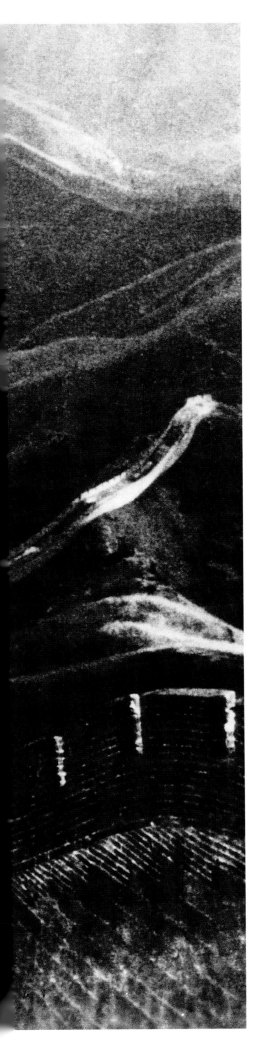

"I LEARNED ENOUGH TO KNOW THAT MAN DID NOT KNOW EVERYTHING THERE WAS TO KNOW ABOUT LIFE, AND IN MY OPINION THAT NEITHER EAST NOR WEST, THE SPIRITUAL AND THE MATERIAL, HAD ANY FULL ANSWER."

L. RON HUBBARD

1928: Near Nan-k'ou Pass, west of Peking.
Photograph by L. Ron Hubbard.

Peking; circa 1928: At the gates to the Forbidden City.
Photograph by L. Ron Hubbard.

ADVENTURES & EXPLORATIONS

Adventure is my guidon," declared L. Ron Hubbard, and promptly proceeded to etch that statement across, not only land and sea, but also, very boldly, across the skies.

It all began one mid-April morning in 1931, not long after his return from the Pacific. Having entered a pedestrian George Washington University (or so it must have seemed after Peking), he joined Engineering Dean, Arthur F. Johnson and a few "air minded youths" for gliding lessons at Washington's Congressional Airfield. The craft was a decidedly dangerous Franklin utility glider, and facilities were primitive: a ramshackle tower above patches of knee-high grass and ankle-deep mud, a corrugated shed for the hanger. Nevertheless, as Ron was soon asking: "What sort of mesmerism does a glider exercise that it makes a man eat, sleep, talk and fly until he is on the verge of a breakdown?" Thereafter, and when not breaking sustained powerless flight records, Ron "Flash" Hubbard, as journalists of the day soon dubbed him, could be regularly seen "thumbing his nose at the undertakers who used to come out to the field and titter."

If less obviously dangerous, Ron's Caribbean voyages through these years were certainly no less adventurous. The first, dubbed the Caribbean Motion Picture Expedition, launched in June 1932, from Baltimore, Maryland. The vessel was the *Doris Hamlin*. Her crew consisted of some fifty university students, with barely a league of experience among them, and head winds out of the Chesapeake Bay nearly shredded the sails. But what an altogether "rousing voyage to pirate-haunted isles and voodoo-cursed villages," as one of the party exclaimed.

The second Caribbean adventure of the season, commencing in October of 1932, was the West Indies Mineralogical Expedition. As the title implies, the stated aim was the survey and mining of precious deposits—or as Ron himself described it, "picking fabulous float from rivers which glittered with gold and silver." In fact, however, that "fabulous float" lay well beyond arm's reach, and Ron was soon reporting from deep within the Puerto Rican jungle. In the end, however, and quite in addition to the photographs to follow, he not only managed a sizable haul of manganese and silica, but actually the island's first complete mineralogical survey under United States dominion.

Dubbed the Alaskan Radio Experimental Expedition, and carrying the coveted flag of the Explorers Club, Ron's 1940 expedition saw not only his recharting of a treacherous inside passage to Alaska, but the testing of a then novel Radio Direction Finder. Described as the first real navigational improvement since the sextant, this Radio Direction Finder stands as the linear antecedent to the LORAN (LOng RAnge Navigation) system.

For all that device offered, however, this 1940 Alaskan Radio Experimental Expedition aboard a thirty-two-foot ketch proved nothing if not eventful. Among other trying moments came engine failures amidst thirty foot waves and an absolutely hellish passage through a raging gauntlet known as the Seymour Narrows—all while snapping rolls of thirty-five-millimeter film with a stereoptical lens for three-dimensional detail. Yet as also suggested by those photographs, and as Ron himself so succinctly put it, "What is life without challenge?"

Washington, DC; 1931: L. Ron Hubbard, as one reporter wrote, "He just dared the ground to come up and hit him."

*San Diego, California; 1933:
One of the many air meets Ron
covered as a roving correspondent
for* The Sportsman Pilot.
Photograph by L. Ron Hubbard.

*Winners of the "Langley Day" air
meet at Washington DC's College
Park Airport, May 1933.
Photograph by L. Ron Hubbard.*

Port Huron, Michigan; September 1931: Suitably equipped in their LeBlond-powered Arrow Sport, Ron "Flash" Hubbard and Phil "Flip" Browning set off on a barnstorming adventure, "With the wind as our only compass."

1933: Photograph by L. Ron Hubbard for The Sportsman Pilot.

Ron's flying helmet bearing the Japanese characters for "Good Luck."

53

1934: The experimental Ryan ST, a then high-performance brainchild of Claude Ryan, designer of the Spirit of St. Louis. Ron photographed this craft for his aptly titled Sportsman Pilot article: "Whatever they call it, it just grins."

1931: Out of college, into the sky.

Washington, DC; 1931: "We had no idea of what we would encounter, but we knew from past experience that our plane would get us out." – L. Ron Hubbard

"I STUDIED TO BE A CIVIL ENGINEER IN COLLEGE. I SAW INSTANTLY THAT A CIVIL ENGINEER HAD TO STAY FAR TOO LONG IN FAR TOO FEW PLACES AND SO I RAPIDLY FORGOT MY CALCULUS AND SLIP STICK AND BEGAN TO PLOT WAYS AND MEANS TO AVOID THE CONTINUANCE OF MY EDUCATION. I DECIDED ON AN EXPEDITION INTO THE CARIBBEAN."

L. RON HUBBARD

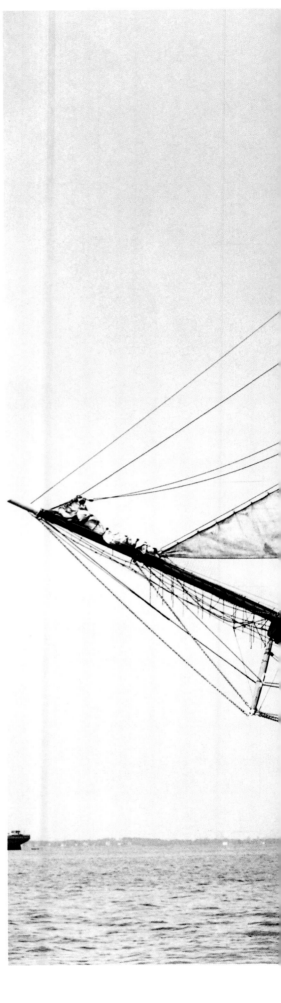

Baltimore, Maryland; 1932: The Doris Hamlin dockside where Ron and his fifty students set their sights on the Caribbean.

Washington, DC; 1932: Director of the famed Caribbean Motion Picture Expedition.

1932: The Doris Hamlin weathering yet another storm. Photograph by L. Ron Hubbard.

Chesapeake Bay, Maryland; 1932: Fifty college students answering ads for "restless young men with wanderlust," set out aboard this last of the great four-masted schooners.

Puerto Rico; 1932: Ron and fellow adventurer, Paul Wilkerson.

November 1932: The first sluice of the West Indies Mineralogical Expedition near San Juan, Puerto Rico. Photograph by L. Ron Hubbard.

1932: The rugged and ultimately disappointing hills near Corozal. Photograph by L. Ron Hubbard.

"TO GO GOLD PROSPECTING IN THE WAKE OF THE CONQUISTADORS, ON THE HUNTING GROUNDS OF THE PIRATES IN THE ISLANDS WHICH STILL REEK OF COLUMBUS IS ROMANTIC, AND I DO NOT BEGRUDGE THE SWEAT WHICH SPLASHED IN THE MUDDY RIVERS, AND THE BITS OF KHAKI WHICH HAVE PROBABLY BLOWN AWAY FROM THE THORN BUSHES LONG AGO."

L. RON HUBBARD

*Near the Barrio del Carmen, Puerto Rico; 1933:
As inland trails grew rougher, mules replaced the
horses. Photograph by L. Ron Hubbard.*

*Corozal, Puerto Rico; 1932: Expedition headquarters in the mountains southwest of San Juan, where five
alluvial-bearing rivers meet. Photograph by L. Ron Hubbard.*

Puerto Rico; 1933:
Photograph by L. Ron Hubbard.

"LAST NIGHT
I WAS UP AT THE EXPLORERS
CLUB AND HAD A NICE TIME.
WILKINS AND STEFANSSON
AND ARCHBOLD AND AD
INFINITUM WERE THERE AND
THEY MADE ME MUCH AT HOME."

L. RON HUBBARD

With Ron's completion of the West Indies Mineralogical Expedition, ethnological studies and aerial mapping from the Arrow Sport, he received his invitation to join the ranks of the exceptional few as a member of the world renowned Explorers Club. Headquartered in New York City and home to the likes of Admiral Byrd and Sir Edmund Hillary, the Explorers Club has provided logistical support for some of the twentieth century's most daring expeditions, very much including L. Ron Hubbard's 1940 voyage to Alaska.

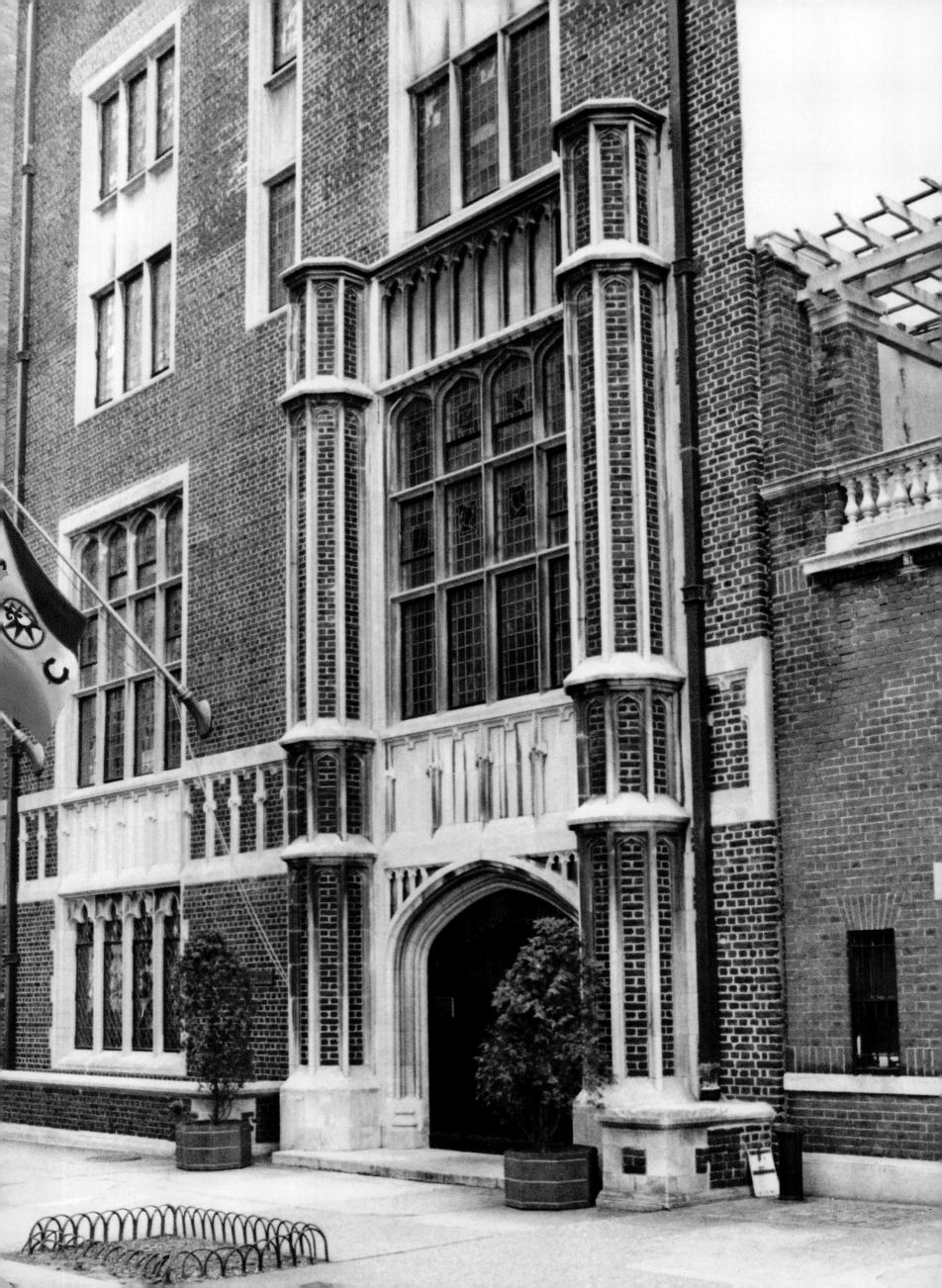

*A selection of correspondence from Ron's
forty-five-year relationship with the Explorers Club.*

*Appropriately, Ron's first description
of his exploration into the human mind
was published in the Explorers Journal.*

The Explorers Journal

COPYRIGHT 1950, BY THE EXPLORERS CLUB

VOL. XXVIII   NEW YORK, WINTER-SPRING, 1950   No. 1

TERRA INCOGNITA: THE MIND

BY L. RON HUBBARD

Probably the strangest place an explorer can go is inside. The earth's frontiers are being rapidly gobbled up by the fleet flight of planes, the stars are not yet reached. But there still exists a dark unknown which, if a strange horizon for an adventurer, is nevertheless capable of producing some adventures scarcely rivaled by Livingstone.

During the course of three minor expeditions before the war the realization came about that one of the most dangerous risks in the field of exploration is not located in the vicinity of the geographical goal, but is hard by from the first moment of planning until the last of disbanding–the unbalanced member of the party.

After some years of war it became even more of a conviction that there are some things more dangerous than the kamikaze, just as they had been more dangerous than malaria.

For a mathematician and navigator to become involved in the complexities of the mental frontiers is not particularly strange; to produce something like results from his explorations into the further realms of the unknown definitely is.

There is no reason here to become expansive on the subject of Dianetics. The backbone of the science can be found where it belongs, in the textbook and in professional publications on the mind and body.

But in that Dianetics was evolved because of observations in exploration for the purpose of bettering exploration results and safeguarding the success of expeditions, it would be strange, indeed, to make no mention of it in its proper generative field.

Based on heuristic principles and specifically on the postulate that the mission of life is survival and that the survival is in several lines rather than merely one, Dianetics contains several basic axioms which seem to approximate natural laws. But regardless of what it approximates, it works. Man surviving as himself, as his progeny, as his group or race, is still surviving equally well. The mechanisms of his body and his society are evidently intended to follow this axiom since, by following it in a scientific manner, several other discoveries came about. That Dianetics is of interest to medicine–in that it apparently conquers and cures all psychosomatic ills and that it is of interest to institutions where it has a salutary effect upon the insane–is beyond the province of its original intention.

What was wanted was a therapy which could be applied by expedition commanders or doctors which would work easily and in all cases to restore rationale to party members unduly affected by hardship and, more important, which would provide a yardstick in the selection of personnel which would obviate potential mental and physical failure. That goal was gained and when gained was found to be relatively simple.

It was discovered that the human mind has not been too well credited for its actual ability. Rather than a weak and capricious organ, it was found to be inherently capable of amazing strength and stamina and that one of its primary purposes was to be right and always right. The normal mind can be restored to the optimum mind rather easily, but that is again beside the point.

The focus of infection of mental and psychosomatic ills was discovered in a hidden but relatively accessible place. During moments when the conscious mind (Dianetically, the analytical mind) is suspended in operation–by injury, anesthesia, illness such as delirium–there is a more fundamental level still in operation, still recording. Anything said to a man when he is unconscious from pain or shock is registered in its entirety. It then operates, on the return of consciousness, as a posthypnotic suggestion, with the additional menace of holding in the body the pain of the incident. The content of the moment or period of unconsciousness is called, Dianetically, a *comanome* (Greek–"unconscious law"). The words contained in the comanome are like commands, hidden but powerful when restimulated by an analogous situation in later life. The pain in the comanome becomes the psychosomatic illness. Any perceptic in the comanome is capable of reviving some of the strength of that comanome when it is observed in the environment. The comanome so planted in the mind has its content of perceptics–smell, sound, sight, tactile, organic sensations. It has them in a precise order. The comanome can be played off like a drama when awake life perceptics restimulate it. Which is to say that for every perceptic in the comanome there are a variety of equivalents in awake environment. A man becomes weary, sees one or more of the perceptics in his surroundings and becomes subject to the comanome within him.

For example, a man falls into a crevasse and is knocked out. His companions haul him forth. One is angry and comments over the unconscious man that he was always a clumsy fool and that the party would be better off without him. Another member defends the unconscious man, saying he is a good fellow. The unconscious man received a blow on the head in his fall and his arm was slightly injured in the recovery.

After regaining consciousness the injured man has no "memory" of the incident, which is to say, he cannot recall it consciously. The incident may lie dormant and never become active. But, for our example, the man who criticized him one day says, at the moment when the formerly injured man is weary, that somebody is a clumsy fool. Unreasonably, the formerly injured man

will become intensely antagonistic. He will also feel an unreasonable friendship for the man who spoke up for him. Now the comanome is "keyed in" or has become a part of the subject's "behavior pattern." The next time the injured man is on ice, the sight of it makes his head ache and his arm hurt in dwindling ratio to how tired he gets. Further, he may pick up a chronic headache or arthritis in his arm, the injuries being continually restimulated by such things as the smell of his parka, the presence of the other members, etc., etc.

That is a comanome at work. How far it is capable of reducing a man's efficiency is a matter of many an explorer's log. A case of malaria can be restimulated. A man has malaria in a certain environment. Now having had it he becomes far more susceptible to malaria *psychosomatically* in that same environment and with those people who tended him. He can become a serious drag on the party, for each new slight touch restimulates the old one and what should have been a mild case is a highly painful one, being the first case of malaria plus all the subsequent cases. Malaria is a bug. As a bug it can be handled. As a comanome it will defy cure, for there is no Atabrine for comanomes short of their removal.

Almost all serious comanomes occur early in life–amazingly early. The early ones form a basic structure to which it is very simple to append later comanomes. Comanomes can wait from childhood to be "keyed in" and active at 25, 50, 70 years of age.

The comanome, a period of unconsciousness which contained physical pain and apparent antagonism to the survival of the individual, has been isolated as the sole source of mental aberration. A certain part of the mind seems to be devoted to their reception and retention. In Dianetics, this part of the mind is called the *reactive mind*. From this source, without otherwise disclosing themselves, the comanomes act upon the body and cause the body to act in society in certain patterns. The reactive mind is alert during periods when the analytical mind–or conscious mind–is reduced in awareness.

It is a matter of clinical proof that the persistency, ambition, drive, willpower and personal force are in no degree dependent upon

Ron's Explorers Club bracelet.

British Columbia; December 1940: Alaska bound.
Photograph by L. Ron Hubbard.

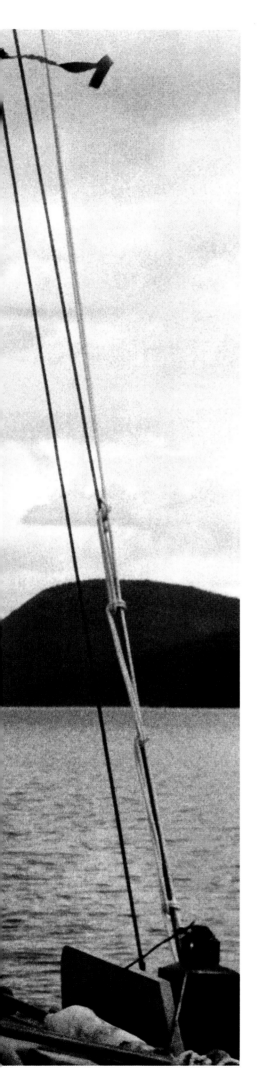

"Alone, wet, hungry, hand cramped upon a tiller, a sailor knows more truth in those hours than all mankind in his millions of years."

L. Ron Hubbard

Puget Sound, Washington; Spring 1940: Test trials for the Magician, soon to embark on the Alaskan Radio Experimental Expedition.

Seattle, Washington; Spring 1940: The Magician, prior to modifications. Ron later removed the aft mast to improve ease of handling. Photograph by L. Ron Hubbard.

Off British Columbian coast; December 1940: One of hundreds of photographs Ron provided to the US Navy's Hydrographic Office for the accurate charting of these waters.

Main Street, Ketchikan, Alaska; 1940.

*Fish Creek, Ketchikan;
November 1940:
Indian boys fishing for salmon
using large poles with a hook
at the end to spear the fish.
Photograph by L. Ron
Hubbard.*

*The Magician docked in Ketchikan's Thomas Basin, with the Explorers
Club flag attached to the top of the mainmast. Photograph by L. Ron
Hubbard.*

British Columbian coastline; December 1940:
Photograph by L. Ron Hubbard.

Ketchikan; 1940: Home to roustabouts, loggers and hardy sportsmen.
Photograph by L. Ron Hubbard.

Prince Rupert, British Columbia: "In from the banks and taking the family out for an airing and a buying spree," wrote Ron of this shot.

Thomas Basin, Ketchikan; October 1940:
The Bird Man.
Photograph by L. Ron Hubbard.

Port of Ketchikan, Alaska; 1940: This large commercial fishing vessel worked for the local cannery—the only fish cannery on Alaska's Panhandle. Photograph by L. Ron Hubbard.

Ketchikan, Alaska; November 1940: Native Alaskan musicians and singers who performed Ron's ballads and chanteys at Radio KGBU. Photograph by L. Ron Hubbard.

THROUGH HELL
AND HIGH WATER

By Members of
THE EXPLORERS CLUB

ROBERT M. MCBRIDE & COMPANY
New York

An early LRH account of his Alaskan adventures in the Explorers Club book, Through Hell and High Water.

IT BEARS TELLING

BY CAPTAIN L. RON HUBBARD

I WISH BILL MANN WAS here today. All that expansion at his Zoo in Washington has kept him too closely confined and we don't see enough of him around the Long Table.

There is one question I particularly wanted to ask him. I wanted to know if it was possible for a man to wrestle with a full-grown Kodiak bear and come out on top. I have heard that they are rather unrefined and that most people have been advised to stay away from them. Yet there is a persistent rumor around town that our redheaded Captain Ron Hubbard goes out of his way to pick wrestling matches with Kodiaks. It has even reached the point where ballads are being written about his prowess.

Now, Captain Hubbard left these parts recently on a supposedly scientific expedition. He was even allowed to carry the Club flag, which meant that his purpose was scientific. His schooner Magician was well equipped to carry on some badly needed radio studies and research, but we haven't heard anything about that. Bears are all we hear about.

Have you anything to say for yourself, Ron?

GENTLEMEN, NOT EVEN HERE AM I SAFE FROM THIS CONTINUAL CHATTER about bears. I am getting so I can't—oops, I almost made that horrible pun which has been following me about.

To begin, the whole thing is a damned lie. I did not make love to the bear and the bear did not die of longing. Further, I do not make a practice of going around picking on poor, innocent Kodiak bears. The day I arrived in New York City, this thing began: I picked up my phone to hear a cooing voice say, "Cap'n do you like to wrassle with bears?" And since that day I have had no peace. How the story arrived ahead of me I do not know. Personally I tried hard to keep it a dark—I mean the whole thing is a damned lie!

A man can spend endless months of hardship and heroic privation in checking coast pilots; he can squeeze his head to half its width between earphones calculating radio errors; he can brave storm and sudden death in all its most horrible forms in an attempt to increase man's knowledge, and what happens? Is he a hero? Do people look upon his salt-encrusted and exhausted self with awe? Do universities give him degrees and governments commissions? NO! They all look at him with a giggle and ask him if he likes to wrassle with bears. It's an outrage! It's enough to make a man take up paper-doll cutting! Gratitude, bah! Attention and notoriety have centered upon one singular accident—an exaggerated untruth—and the gigantic benefit to the human race are all forgotten!

Gentlemen, examine the facts. A Kodiak bear, known in Alaska as the "brownie," is the world's largest carnivorous animal. He stands as tall as two of us and weighs sixteen hundred active and ferocious pounds.

Ketchikan, Alaska; 1940: Ron broadcasting from Ketchikan's KGBU radio station, where he not only hosted "The Mail Buoy" program, but also performed ballads of his own composition and sponsored a writer's contest.

"ALASKAN RADIO EXPERIMENTAL EXPEDITION: MY OWN PURPOSE ON THIS IS NOT REMARKED. IT WAS TO LOOK INTO THE ALEUT AND TLINGIT INDIANS AS WELL AS THE HAIDAS, THE LAST BEING VERY CLOSE TO THE WHITE RACE. I WAS PARTICULARLY VERY INTERESTED IN THEIR STORIES AND LEGENDS CONCERNING THE GREAT FLOOD, HAVING FOUND THIS LEGEND IN ALMOST ANY PRIMITIVE RACE I HAVE MET."

L. RON HUBBARD

The Magician; *December 1940: Heading home to Seattle.*

Ketchikan, Alaska; November 1940: Having charted numerous coves and inlets for the United States Navy, while field-testing advanced navigational tools, L. Ron Hubbard became Ketchikan's most celebrated mariner. (On LRH's right wrist appears his Explorers Club bracelet.)

THE GOLDEN AGE OF FICTION

My salvation," Ron proclaimed, "is to write, write and write some more. To pile up copy, stack up stories, roll the wordage and generally conduct my life along the one line of success I have ever had. I write."

And write he did. Working at a truly legendary pace through the bleakest years of the Great Depression, L. Ron Hubbard forever established himself in the ranks of popular fiction. His primary outlet was the now fabled pulps—so named for the pulpwood stock on which they were printed—and easily the most popular vehicle of the era. If first and foremost an every man's publication, the likes of *Argosy, Astounding, Black Mask* and *Five Novels Monthly* were by no means without merit. Indeed, quite in addition to L. Ron Hubbard, readers were regularly treated to Raymond Chandler, Dashiell Hammett, Robert Heinlein and Edgar Rice Burroughs—to name but a few who found their literary feet in the pulps.

Although generally best remembered for fantasies and science fiction, in fact Ron wrote in no particular genre. Or more precisely he wrote in all: adventure, mystery, western, even romance. He also, of course, wrote for the silver screen, most notably Columbia Pictures' *The Secret of Treasure Island.* Then, too, and as implied, he wrote fast, with a regular production of a hundred thousand words a month in but three days a week. Hence, *Standard* magazine editor Jack Schiff's remark: If you needed a story on a Monday, you only had to telephone Ron Hubbard on a Friday.

But as also implied, the real hallmark of these days were the LRH stories themselves. "As perfect a piece of science fiction as has ever been written," declared Robert Heinlein of Ron's *Final Blackout,* while even fifty years later horror master Stephen King described Ron's *Fear* as "One of the few books in the chiller genre which actually merits employment of the overworked adjective 'classic,' as in 'This is a classic tale of creeping surreal menace and horror.'" Then there was his equally classic *Ole Doc Methuselah* tales of an intergalactic physician; and his tribute to Blackfeet nobility, *Buckskin Brigades.*

When considering the photographic record of these days, however, the issue is not so much what he wrote, but where. In the main, Ron divided his time between two homes. The first stood in Port Orchard, Washington above Puget Sound. Aptly dubbed "The Hilltop," it commanded a magnificent view of a generally mist-shrouded Sound, and distant Mount Rainier beyond. In addition to the Hilltop proper, and with profits from Hollywood screenplays, Ron had built his writer's cabin—replete with airtight stove that tended to hiss like breaking surf and a bunk like something from a sailing ship.

When not ensconced in his Hilltop cabin, Ron could generally be found in that literary mecca which has always beckoned writers, New York City. Actual places of residence varied: a basement apartment in Greenwich Village, another on Riverside Drive and an eighth-floor suite in the Knickerbocker Hotel. In the final analysis, however, it was New York itself that was home—the manuscript-cluttered offices of agents and editors, the atmospheric watering holes of such pals as Lester "Doc Savage" Dent and Walter "The Shadow" Gibson, the otherwise ordinary restaurants where Ron convened as president of the American Fiction Guild on Friday afternoons, and, finally, all else that allowed him "to write, write and write some more."

South Pacific; circa 1929:
"The writer who has drawn much from the world will find that his mind is filled with material." – L. Ron Hubbard

Washington, DC; circa 1931:
An author at the start of a fifty-year career.

Ron's award-winning one-act play, The God Smiles, from May 1932.

Helena, Montana; 1928: As a Nugget staff writer. Ron stands second row from top, center.

Washington, DC; 1931: With fraternity brothers at George Washington University, Ron, second from right.

As a seasoned professional by 1935, Ron was regularly called upon to pass along tips for novice writers in journals like these.

Washington, DC; circa 1931:
In addition to duties as a reporter to the Washington Herald, Ron also scripted radio dramas and performed ballads.

New York City; 1936:
L. Ron Hubbard (center, second row) as president of the American Fiction Guild.

Balboa Park, San Diego, California; circa 1934:
Where Ron first commenced, "to pile up copy, stack up stories,
roll the wordage."

"An enthusiasm, even a freshness and sparkle, decidedly rare in this type of romance." New York Times Book Review, in reply to Ron's first novel, 1937.

San Diego, California; circa 1934:
"I wrote to the best of my ability and with great
sincerity." – L. Ron Hubbard

San Diego, California; circa 1934:
"Several of you have wondered how L. Ron Hubbard gets the splendid color which always characterizes his stories of faraway places. The answer is, he's been there."
Note to readers from Thrilling Adventures editor.

*Hollywood, California;
circa 1935:
The writers complex at
Columbia Studios where
Ron scripted* The Secret
of Treasure Island.

With a production rate of some fifty scenes a day, Ron's talents were much in demand. Here are posters from but some of the films he helped script through the summer of 1937.

San Diego, California; circa 1934.

New York City; circa 1938:
Portrait of L. Ron Hubbard whose name
(or his various pen names) had appeared on the
covers of more than thirty different publications
for a total of some fifteen million words by 1950.

John W. Campbell, Jr. (above right),
Street & Smith editor. So taken
was Campbell with Ron's works of
fantasy that he launched an entirely
new publication exclusively devoted
to that genre: Unknown.
Among other classic LRH stories
first appearing in the pages of
Unknown were Typewriter in the
Sky and Fear—works that eventually
led Campbell to inform Ron:
"The field of fantasy has been
preempted by you."

Port Orchard, Washington; circa 1936:
Home from New York.

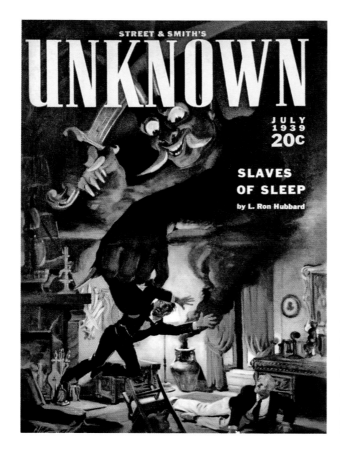

As a leading author from Science Fiction's Golden Age, Ron helped reshape the genre with timeless stories such as his Slaves of Sleep and Ole Doc Methuselah.

Between 1934 and 1950,
L. Ron Hubbard wrote more than
fifteen million words of
fiction, in over two hundred classic
publications, some of which are
shown here.
To span the many genres for which
he wrote, Ron employed more
than two dozen pseudonyms, some
of which are listed below:

WINCHESTER REMINGTON COLT

LT. JONATHAN DALY

CAPT. CHARLES GORDON

CAPT. L. RON HUBBARD

BERNARD HUBBEL

MICHAEL KEITH

RENE LAFAYETTE

LEGIONNAIRE 148

LEGIONNAIRE 14830

KEN MARTIN

SCOTT MORGAN

LT. SCOTT MORGAN

KURT VON RACHEN

BARRY RANDOLPH

CAPT. HUMBERT REYNOLDS

JOHN SEABROOK

Snake River, Grand Teton National Park, Wyoming; circa 1936.

"My main forte was adventure when I did get into fiction, as I had a considerable fund of information. My output was about one hundred thousand words per month. I was often hard put to find enough market, thus I wrote under about five different styles and five different lines of fiction to any and all magazines then being published. I sold ninety-four percent of what I wrote, first draft, first submission."

L. RON HUBBARD

"The Old Mill," as Ron affectionately dubbed his Remington.

95

POSTSCRIPT

In the summer of 1980, in what amounted to his first "spare time" in decades, Ron commenced work on a novel that would forever place him at the forefront of popular fiction. Described as "pure science fiction," and written in celebration of his fiftieth anniversary as a professional writer, this was *Battlefield Earth: A Saga of the Year 3000*. At almost a half-a-million words, it stands as the largest epic of the genre, and was likewise the most popular. Indeed, it proved a monumental bestseller in fifteen nations worldwide, earned both the Academy of Science Fiction Fantasy and Horror Films' Golden Scroll Award and Saturn Award, and otherwise lives on as the single most memorable work of its kind.

Equally memorable, and no less acclaimed was Ron's next work of fiction, the ten volume, 1.2 million word *Mission Earth* series. A wry satire of universal dimensions, *Mission Earth* not only earned broad critical acclaim (Ron was the first non-Italian, for example, to receive Italy's coveted Nova Science Fiction Award), but also proved matchlessly popular. Point of fact: Every one of its ten volumes immediately rose to both *New York Times* and international bestseller lists—a remarkable feat that has never been rivaled in publishing history.

What is finally most remarkable, however, is the sheer rate at which Ron produced the 1.6 million words of *Battlefield Earth* and *Mission Earth* in just under twenty months. For given the average professional generates but six to twelve thousand words a week, it is not for nothing that L. Ron Hubbard has been called the undisputed king of high-speed writers at his twenty thousand words of finished copy every week . . . and at <u>that</u>, as we have said, in <u>spare</u> time between more serious activities. While as for those who would question the quality of prose at such a rate, there is also this to consider: With his combined nonfiction works, Ron enjoyed twenty-one consecutive international bestsellers through the 1980s and 1990s, also a feat unmatched in publishing history.

> *"I've always worked in all the arts. It keeps my hand in, amuses people and whiles away the otherwise idle hour. It's better than playing video games!"*
> — L. Ron Hubbard

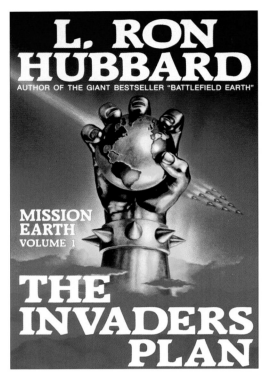

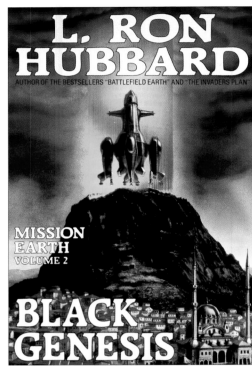

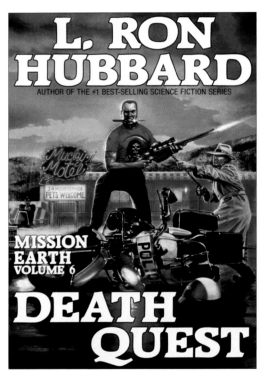

Battlefield Earth *the perennial international bestseller. Thus far, it has been translated into thirteen languages and released in more than fifteen countries. It is without a doubt the most popular single-volume science fiction work of the last two decades. In addition to the book, Ron composed a unique and imaginative music album to accompany the text.* Battlefield Earth, *the album, features thirteen compositions by Ron inspired by characters and significant events from the story.*

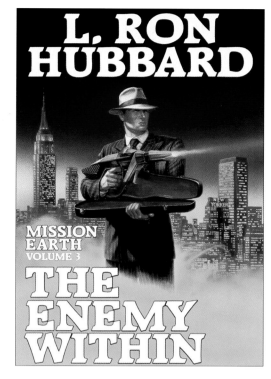

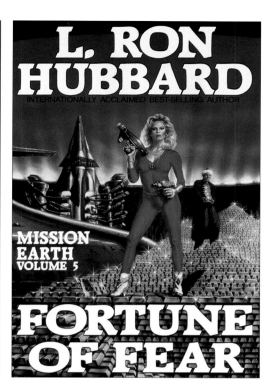

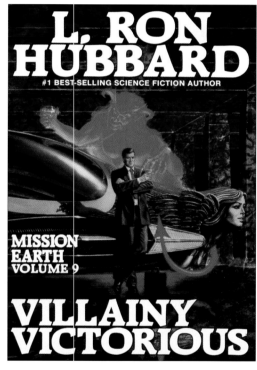

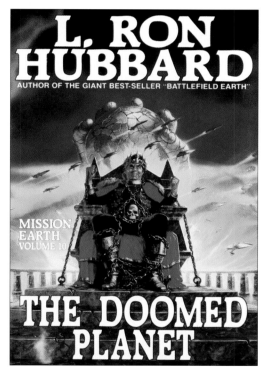

Each volume of the Mission Earth *series was a* New York Times *bestseller. It has been released in twelve countries and has sold more than seven million copies in six languages. It is also accompanied by its own "soundtrack" with lyrics and music by L. Ron Hubbard.*

The Birth of Dianetics & Scientology

For nearly a quarter of a century," wrote L. Ron Hubbard, "I have been engaged in the investigation of the fundamentals of life, the material universe and human behavior." And if no camera could possibly record such a journey ("down many highways, through many byroads, into many back alleys of uncertainty," as he explained) the images would still seem to tell us much.

For example, there is the hulking *USS Algol* off the west coast where, in 1944, he first began the application of early Dianetics procedures on victims of war neurosis. There is the Oak Knoll Naval Hospital in Northern California where, against all odds, he used those same procedures to save the lives of former prisoners of Japanese internment camps. Then there is the 1947 Hollywood clinic where he further tested procedures on members of the film community, the literal back alleys of Los Angeles where he studied pathological behavior, the Pasadena emergency wards where he treated trauma victims, the Georgia institution where he worked the severely insane . . . all to the benefit of some three hundred men and women, and all before finally retiring to a Washington, DC apartment to conclude: "Dianetics offers the first anatomy of the human mind and techniques for handling the hitherto unknown reactive mind, which causes irrational and psychosomatic behavior. It has successfully removed any compulsions, repressions, neuroses and psychoses to which it has been applied."

Images from the first weeks of May 1950 and the release of *Dianetics: The Modern Science of Mental Health* tell even more: LRH at his home in Elizabeth, New Jersey where he woke one Monday morning to find several dozen readers camped among the hedgerows. LRH at the first Dianetics Foundation where newspapers declared, "Because of its very newness and its abnormally rapid growth to national proportions (with the end no means in sight), Hubbard of necessity is still the whole hub of control and direction and decision." LRH before an audience of six thousand at the Shrine Auditorium in Los Angeles and then again with the first several hundred Los Angeles students. Yet remembering his research had always been a solitary trek wherein, as he wrote, "one must cheer one's own triumphs and weep to himself his despair," there is also the Palm Springs retreat where, with the first pages of a new work entitled *Science of Survival,* he took the next crucial step of discovery in 1951.

Images from the extraordinary months of late 1951, to the founding of Scientology in 1952, can really only hint at the intensity of his journey. For with his entrance into a wholly spiritual realm, as he wrote a colleague of the day, comes phenomena one could hardly even "articulate in language to others." Nevertheless, there is LRH at the Hubbard College in Wichita, Kansas where he very pointedly asked, "Are we knocking on the door of the human soul?" There is LRH in Phoenix, Arizona where early lectures on the subject were delivered in the shadow of Camelback Mountain, and where much of the actual research was conducted against a nightly chorus of coyotes, (which, as he remarked, "add to the flavor of things when you're researching spirits"). Then again, there are the portraits from these days, which quite apart from time and place, would seem to tell us so much about a journey that finally brought him "across the rim of hell and into the very arms of heaven."

"You are beginning an adventure. Treat it as an adventure. And may you never be the same again." – L. Ron Hubbard

"What is generally missed is that my writing financed research to see if I could find a common denominator of existence." – L. Ron Hubbard

The earliest philosophic formulations upon which Dianetics is based are found in Ron's 1938 manuscript "Excalibur."

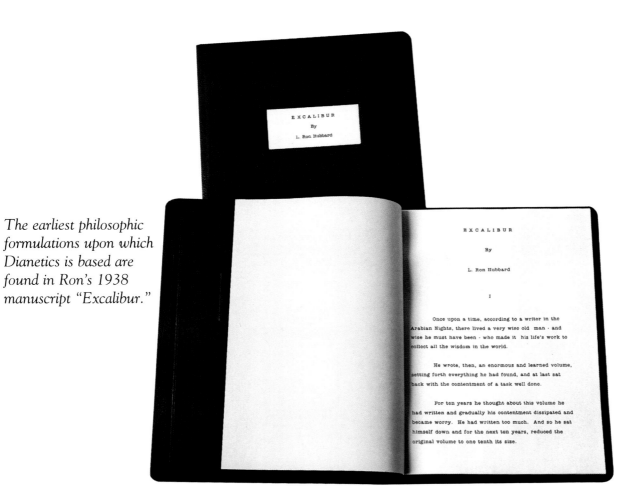

EXCALIBUR

By

L. Ron Hubbard

I

Once upon a time, according to a writer in the Arabian Nights, there lived a very wise old man - and wise he must have been - who made it his life's work to collect all the wisdom in the world.

He wrote, then, an enormous and learned volume, setting forth everything he had found, and at last sat back with the contentment of a task well done.

For ten years he thought about this volume he had written and gradually his contentment dissipated and became worry. He had written too much. And so he sat himself down and for the next ten years, reduced the original volume to one tenth its size.

Port Orchard, Washington; 1938: Ron's cabin where he ventured "into the howling black where no adventurer had groped before."

Portland, Oregon; 1943:
Lt. L. Ron Hubbard as navigation officer of the USS Algol, when despite all else,
he pressed on with research into the plight of the human condition.

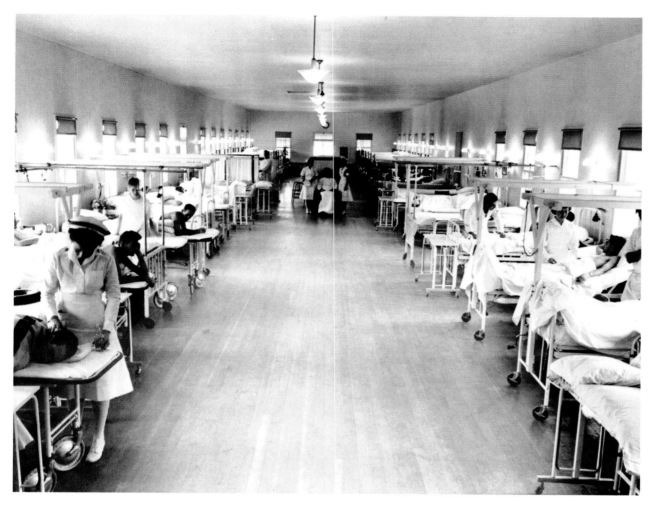

Oak Knoll Naval Hospital,
Oakland, California;
circa 1945:
Among the five thousand
patients here were the first
eleven "test cases" for early
Dianetics procedures.
All eleven, seriously suffering
from war-related illness, were
returned to health, and in this
way, Ron reported, "I put
together guidelines for further
research."

*Morro Bay, near San Luis Obispo,
California; circa 1948:
It was here, on the heels of his Oak Knoll
tests, that Ron paused to compile notes on
links between mental trauma and physical
disabilities.*

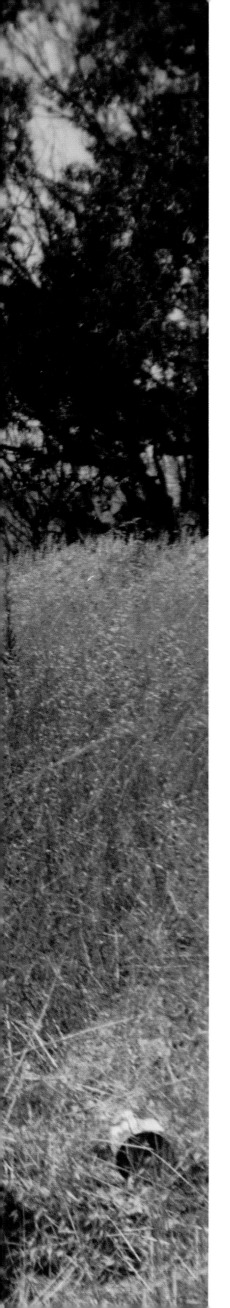

Outside Los Angeles, California; circa 1947:
With the essentials of a workable therapy now in place, Ron set out to test that therapy from all walks of life.

St. Joseph's Hospital, Savannah, Georgia; circa 1948:
As a lay practitioner at this facility, Ron systematically returned forty "charity cases" to full health and sanity with Dianetics.

Washington, DC; circa 1948:
Returning to the nation's capital after the completion of research in Georgia, Ron summarized the discoveries of Dianetics in his "Original Thesis."

The "Original Thesis" published today as The Dynamics of Life.

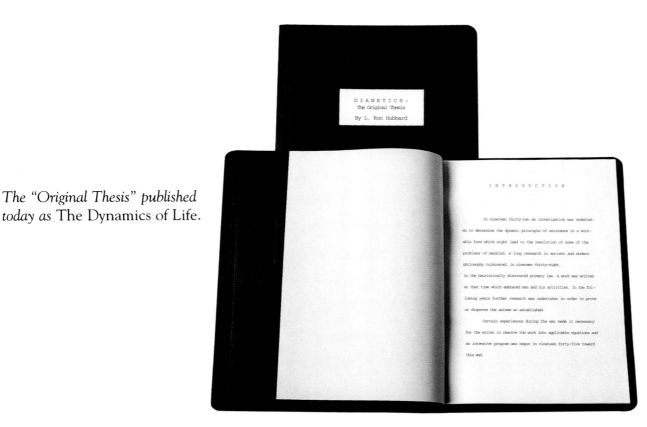

Bayhead, New Jersey; 1949:
Birthplace of "The Book," as readers dubbed it: Dianetics: The Modern Science of Mental Health.

Author of a work that was about to take the "US by storm."

Author and first edition of the all-time best-selling, self-help book.

The New York Times Book Review

SUNDAY, DECEMBER 10, 1950

The Best Sellers

An analysis based on reports from leading book sellers in 36 cities, showing the sales rating of 16 leading fiction and general titles, and their relative standing over the past 3 weeks.

General

Nov. 19	Nov. 26	Dec. 3	This Week	
3	1	2	1	Courtroom *Reynolds*
6	5	1	2	The Little Princesses *Crawford*
4	2	3	3	Look Younger, Live Longer *Hauser*
5	6	5	4	**Dianetics** *Hubbard*
1	4	4	5	Worlds in Collision *Velikovsky*
2	3	6	6	Roosevelt in Retrospect *Gunther*
8	7	7	7	The Mature Mind *Overstreet*
7	8	8	8	John Adams and the American Revolution *Bowen*
12	9	9	9	Behind Closed Doors *Zacharias*
9	10	10	10	Chicago Confidential *Lait and Mortimer*
10	12	14	11	Eleanor of Aquitaine and the Four Kings *Kelly*
		13	12	Springtime in Paris *Paul*
11	11	11	13	Ordeal by Slander *Lattimore*
15	14		14	Mr. Jones, Meet the Master *Marshall*
13	16	12	15	Seeds of Treason *de Toledano and Lasky*
16			16	Escape to Adventure *Maclean*

Los Angeles Times

SELLERS

Nonfiction Leaders
"Dianetics" – Hubbard.
"Look Younger, Live Longer" – Hauser.
"Behind the Flying Saucers" – Scully.
"Courtroom" – Reynolds.
"The Little Princesses" – Crawford.
"The Mature Mind" – Overstreet.
"Worlds in Collision" – Velikovsky.
"The Story of Ernie Pyle" – Miller.
"Betty Crocker's Picture Cook

May Co. and Robinson's.)
Fiction Leaders
"Jubilee Trail" – Bristow.
"The Cardinal" – Robinson.
"Across the River and into the Trees" – Hemingway.
"Floodtide" – Yerby.
"World Enough and Time" – Warren.
"The Spanish Gardener" – Cronin.
"The Egyptian" – Waltari.
"The Wall" – Hersey.

Los Angeles Times

SUNDAY, July 2, 1950 – Part IV 5

TOP BEST SELLERS

IN LOS ANGELES
(From sales records of Broadway, Bullock's, Campbell's, Fowler Bros., May Co. and Robinson's.)
Fiction Leaders
"The Cardinal" – Robinson.
"The Wall" – Hersey.
"Jubilee Trail" – Bristow.
"Star Money" – Winsor.
"The Egyptian" – Waltari.
"Wait for Tomorrow" – Wilder.
"The Plymouth Adventure" – Gebler.
"World Enough and Time" – Warren.
"Sleep Till Noon" – Shulman.
"The Way West" – Guthrie.

Nonfiction Leaders
"Dianetics: The Modern Science of The Mind" – Hubbard.
"The Mature Mind" – Overstreet.
"Look Younger, Live Longer" – Hauser.
"Worlds in Collision" – Velikovsky.
"Seeds of Treason" – Toledano and Lasky.
"Courtroom" – Reynolds.
"Roosevelt in Retrospect" – Gunther.
"The Grand Alliance" – Churchill.
"The Peabody Sisters of Salem" – Tharp.
"The Cocktail Party" – Eliot.

But one of thousands of articles appearing in newspapers across the nation in the first months after May 1950.

DIANETICS: A Door to the Future

by JAMES BLISH

AN increased life span, freedom from 70% of all human illnesses and a major increase in intelligence–these are only a few of the benefits promised us by a new science called "Dianetics."

"Dianetics" is both the name of a recent book about how the human mind operates, and the general term used to cover specific methods of repairing, healing *and perfecting* the human mind.

Just how does the human mind work? Up to a few years ago nobody really knew.

Why does the human mind fail to work efficiently at times, or all the time? Another mystery.

If the claims made for the new science of Dianetics are borne out, both those mysteries are now solved. Some of these claims are so flabbergasting as to stagger even the hardened science-fiction fan. For instance:

Dianetics claims to have cured many types of heart ailment, arthritis, the common cold, stomach ulcers, sinus trouble, asthma, and many other diseases, amounting to about 70% of the whole catalog of human ills.

Dianetics also claims to have cured virtually every known form of mental disease. These cures have encompassed the severest form of insanity, workers in Dianetics declare flatly.

Furthermore–and in this claim (among others) lies Dianetics' bid to be called a science–Dianetics claims to be able to cure all these aberrations and diseases every time, without fail. At the time this is being written, some months before you will read it, Dianetics has been tried on a minimum of 300 people, and, its originators say, has worked 100% without failure in all these cases.

Nor is this all, fantastic though what I've already written may seem to be. Use of Dianetic therapy on so-called "normal" people seems to produce changes in them which can only be described as dynamite.

"Normal" people treated by Dianetic therapy, it's said, undergo a rise in intelligence, efficiency, and well-being averaging a third above their previous capacity! In one case, a woman, the IQ–intelligence quotient–rose *50 points* before the full course of therapy was run!

Such "Clears," as they are called, are said to be immune to any and all forms of mental disease, and to any and all forms of organic diseases caused by mental or emotional difficulties.

It might be a good idea to stop here and ask the names of the people who are making these incredible claims. They are none of them professional quacks, faith-healers, bread-pill rollers, or other forms of swindlers. They are all men with solid reputations, and all, as it happens, quite familiar to the science-fiction reader.

The leader of the new school of thought is L. Ron Hubbard, author of "Fear," "Final Blackout," and many other science-fiction classics. By trade, Hubbard is an engineer.

Hubbard's two principal confreres are John W. Campbell, Jr., and Dr. Joseph E. Winter. Mr. Campbell, of course, is widely known even to the general public as a government consultant in nuclear physics, the author of "The Atomic Story," and to us as the editor of a top-notch science-fiction magazine. Dr. Winter, who by the way is an M.D., not a Ph.D., has published some science-fiction stories; but until Dianetics came along, he was best known as an expert endocrinologist of unimpeachable reputation.

Hubbard's book,* however, does not include any formal evidence for the claims. The Dianetics Institute in Elizabeth, N.J., is equally unwilling to offer authenticated case records or any other evidence of that specific kind. The book, Dianetics men point out, offers the therapy procedures in complete detail. If you want case histories, perform your own experiments.

As it happens, one of the more spectacular cures claimed by Dianetics took place in the New York area, and could be checked from outside sources. Jerome Bixby, editor of PLANET STORIES, checked it. The claim was so; hospital authorities who have no connection with Dianetics as a movement vouch for it, cautiously but definitely.

My own personal tests of the therapy–on myself, my wife, and a friend (namely, Jerome Bixby)–haven't proceeded very far as yet. But as far as they've gone, they check with the claims. The phenomena Hubbard describes in the book do appear. They appear in the order in which he says they appear. And they match his descriptions of them to the letter. Such aftereffects as we've been able to observe also check.

If Dianetics does work–and every check I've been able to run thus far indicates that it does–it may well be the most important discovery of this or any other century. It will bring the long-sought "rule of reason" to the problems of local and world politics, communication, law, and almost every other field of human endeavor–the goal of a 3000 year search.

---

* DIANETICS, by L. Ron Hubbard. Hermitage House, New York, 1950; $4.00. Hermitage, by the way, is the publisher of a number of books on psychology and psychoanalysis universally acknowledged to be serious contributions to the field.

As Ron appeared in the six-part Daily News *series.*

DIANETICS SERIES TODAY IN DAILY NEWS

One of the most controversial subjects of recent months–the new science of Dianetics–is comprehensively analyzed in the language of the layman, starting today in the Daily News.

A Daily News staff writer, with instructions to keep an open mind on the subject and make a thorough study of it, read L. Ron Hubbard's best-selling book, interviewed the author and observed classes of instruction.

What he read, what he saw and what he heard he reports today in the first of a series of articles offering an objective analysis of Dianetics.

To be well informed on this popular subject, start reading the series today on Page 2.

Author tells birth of scientific brainchild

(This is the second of a daily series published by the Daily News on the newly formulated science of Dianetics and the technique of mental therapy known as Dianetic processing. The series will continue an objective and impartial report on the claims and accomplishments of L. Ron Hubbard, formulator of scientific axioms of human thought processes which already have attracted millions of adherents.)

By JOHN CLARKE
(Daily News Staff Writer)

L. Ron Hubbard is a onetime engineer, mathematician, philosopher, naval officer and prolific producer of science fiction of the space ship, or fantastic, school of literature.

He is, more, by his own account, an independent thinker and as such a rebel against Authority and Orthodoxy.

He is a man of 39 years, blocky frame, shocks of very red hair, large and mobile features, seemingly endless energy and ready humor.

Energy and humor stand him in good stead, for since the overnight success of his book, "Dianetics," Hubbard has become, in a few swift months, a personality, a national celebrity and the proprietor of the fastest growing "movement" in the United States.

It has, in fact, become a mass movement of the mushroom type, so great are the numbers of its adher-

ture more friendly than to refrain from critical opinion are the recipients of the ample Hubbard patience. He indicates his confidence they'll come around.

Of his detractors, he makes short shrift. They are simply motivated out of ignorance (of Dianetics) which is deplorable (economic) self-interest, which is even more deplorable.

But if medicine men, the book trade, the literary critics, contemporaries in the writing craft, economists, politicians and observers of human phenomena generally have been astounded, appalled or puzzled by the instantaneous appeal and acceptance of Dianetics, Hubbard is astonished least of all.

DIANETICS
New mental science helps to increase rationality, zest for living, claim

(This is the fourth of a daily series published by the Daily News on the newly formulated science of Dianetics and the technique of mental therapy known as Dianetic processing. The series provides an objective and impartial report on the claims and accomplishments of L. Ron Hubbard, formulator of scientific axioms of human thought processes which already have attracted millions of adherents.)

By JOHN CLARKE
(Daily News Staff Writer)

Spectacular success, particularly the sudden variety, does not bring rewards wholly unadulterated by tribulations, irritations and complications previously unexperienced.

L. Ron Hubbard has learned this lesson, if he did not know it before, in he is pleased with explaining what it is.

Almost hourly, by way of illustration, he is called upon to rebuke the misconception that his theories and his conclusions constitute a new religion.

This is the most common of all the false notions about Dianetics which he is called upon to confront and attempt to batter down.

Although he asserts that all human behaviorisms can be accounted for without resort to metaphysics or mysticism, and although he does have a great deal to say about human morals and mores, Hubbard rejects and considers unfair the attempts which have been made to identify or confuse his (scientific) concepts with organized religions, religious philosophies, spiritual beliefs, faiths, cults or deitific venerations.

Hubbard likewise gravely dismisses other unsympathetic misinterpretations of what he is up to.

Dianetics, for example, is not psychiatry, a substitute for psychiatry, the rival or opponent of psychiatry. It is a new and largely independent mental science through which normal people simply can increase their degree of rationality and zest for life by at least one-third.

Nor is Dianetics a blueprint for the revolution of human civilization, although the author sees implications of vast social and economic change, for the better of course, in a world dominated by "clears" or optimum individuals.

Dianetics therapy, furthermore, does not involve either narcosynthesis or

An early 1950 lecture at the first Dianetics Foundation.

Elizabeth, New Jersey; 1950:
Ron's home where readers were literally camping on the
lawn to await Ron's lectures.

At the dictaphone to answer whole mailbags of letters from
readers.

Los Angeles, California;
1950:
The 123-room "casa" of
the first Los Angeles
Dianetics Foundation.

Los Angeles, California; 1950:
Dianetics in application at the
first professional auditor's
course.

Los Angeles, California; 1950:
Students of the first Dianetics course
in Los Angeles.

The Los Angeles Shrine Auditorium where Ron addressed an audience of six thousand on August 10, 1950.

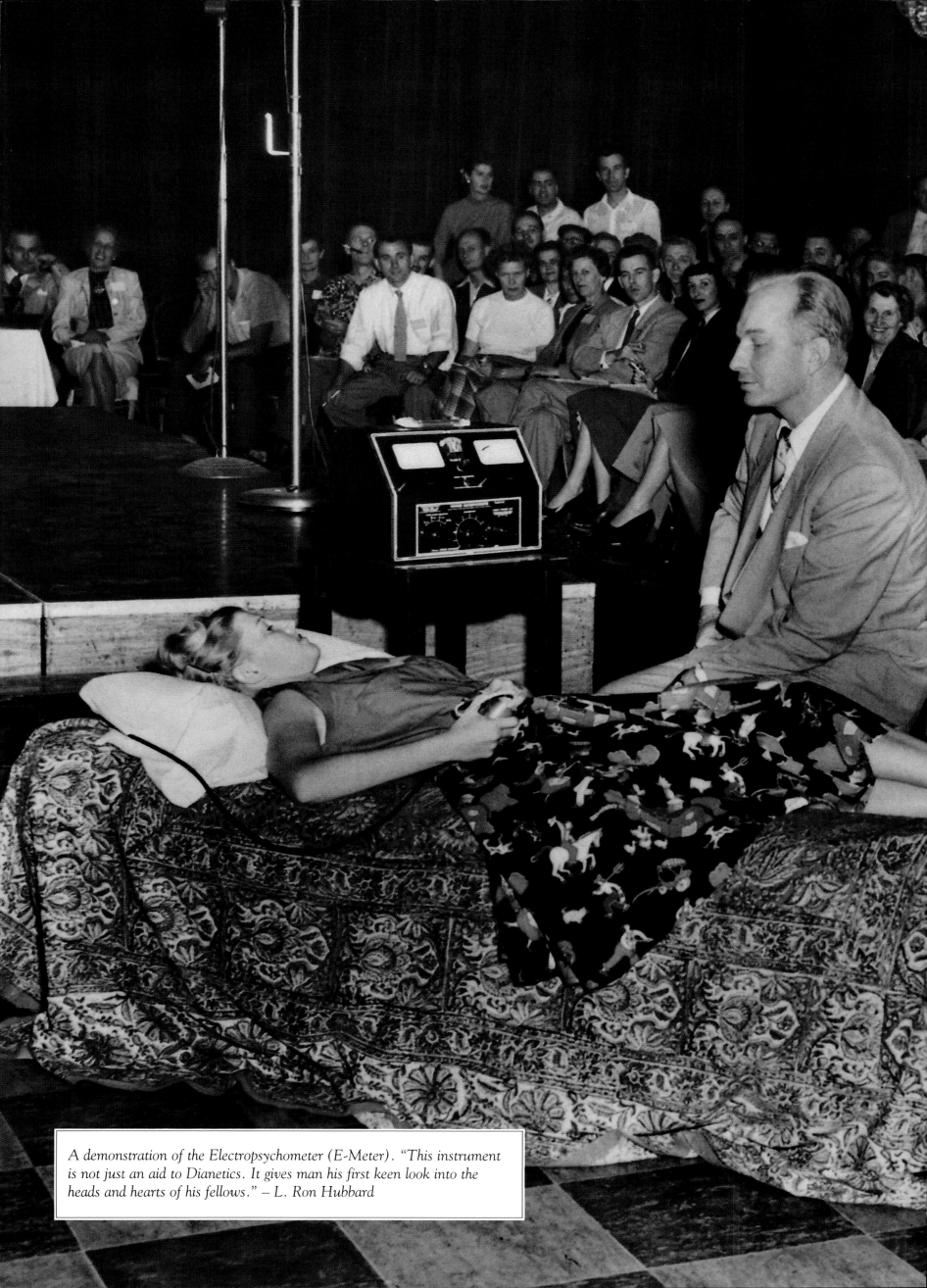

A demonstration of the Electropsychometer (E-Meter). "This instrument is not just an aid to Dianetics. It gives man his first keen look into the heads and hearts of his fellows." – L. Ron Hubbard

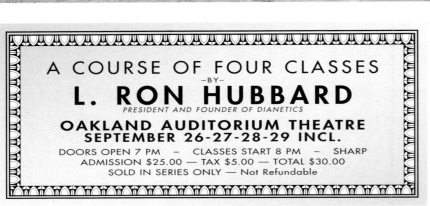

Oakland, California; 1950:
Where notices like this one (left)
packed the house.

Kansas City, Missouri; October 1950:
Entrance to the Kansas City Music Hall where Ron
continued his lecture tour through the "Year of Dianetics."

*Kansas City, Missouri; circa 1950:
Kansas City Music Hall, where Ron
delivered lectures from October 21 to
October 28.*

*Los Angeles, California; 1950:
Ron with staff at the first Los Angeles Foundation.*

121

Palm Springs, California; circa 1951: Where writing commenced on a second Dianetics text, Science of Survival.

Wichita, Kansas; circa 1951:
Site of the Wichita Dianetics Foundation, and research that eventually led from
Ron's pivotal question, "Are we knocking on the door of the human soul?"

Wichita, Kansas; 1951:
Where Science of Survival *was first typeset and published.*

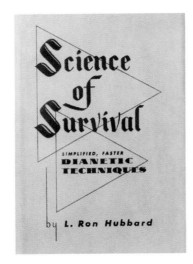

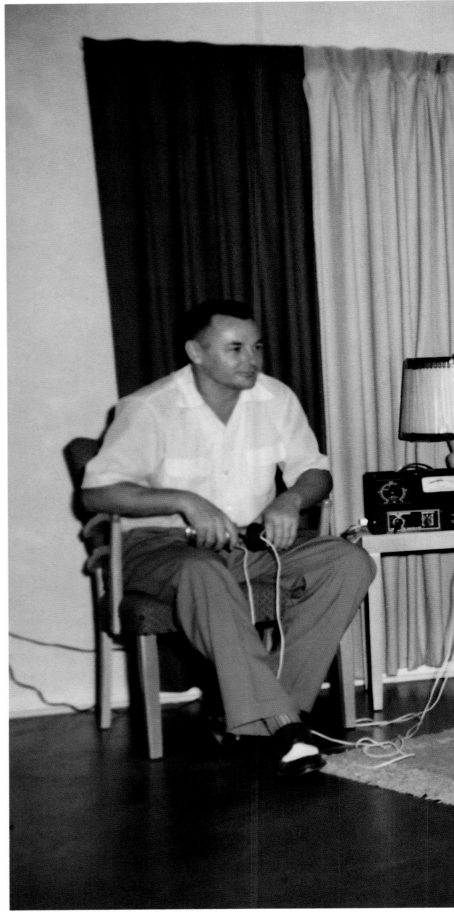

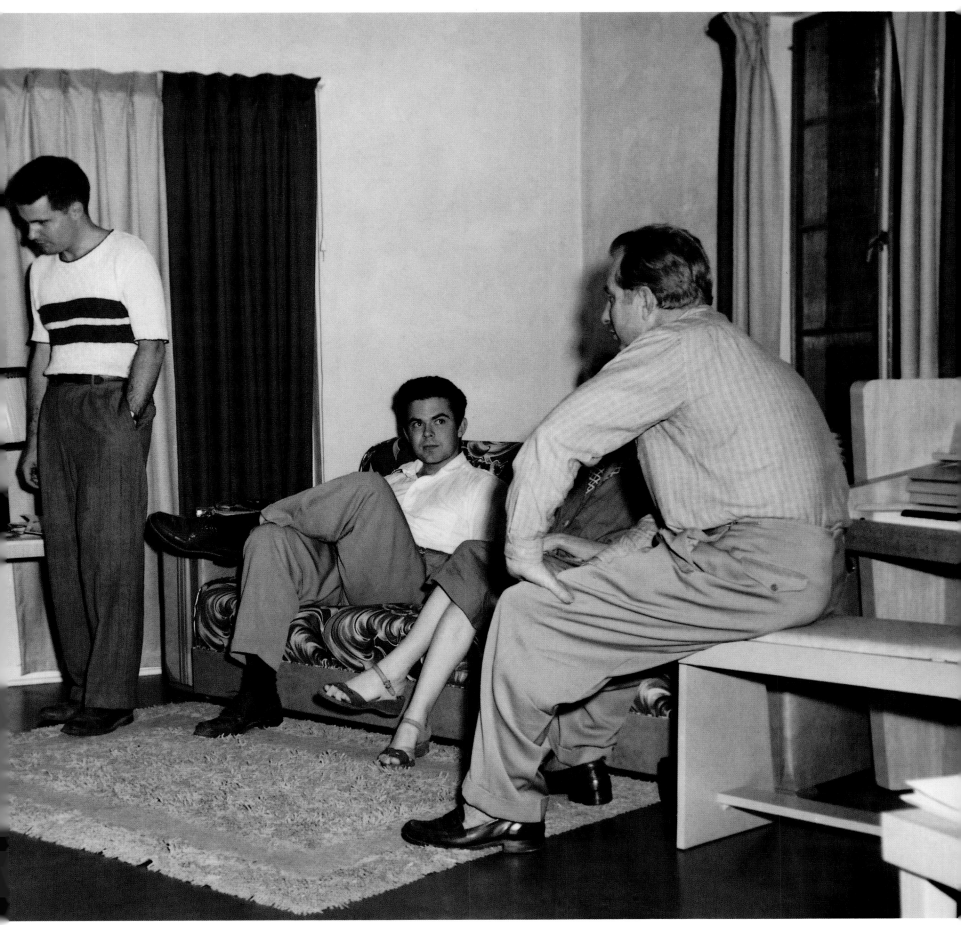

Wichita, Kansas; circa 1951:
A demonstration of the E-Meter at Ron's home on North Yale Street.

Phoenix, Arizona:
Site of research that led to "the isolation,
description and handling of the human spirit."

With the first edition of Self Analysis.

Phoenix, Arizona; 1952:
With the first students and staff at the Office of L. Ron Hubbard.

Phoenix, Arizona; circa 1952:
"We are studying the soul or spirit. We are studying it as itself." – L. Ron Hubbard

"THE TRAIL IS BLAZED,
THE ROUTES ARE SUFFICIENTLY MAPPED FOR
YOU TO VOYAGE IN SAFETY INTO YOUR OWN
MIND AND RECOVER THERE YOUR FULL
INHERENT POTENTIAL, WHICH IS NOT, WE
NOW KNOW, LOW BUT VERY, VERY HIGH."

L. RON HUBBARD

Ron's home near Camelback Mountain.

129

GROWTH OF A RELIGION

Scientology," declared L. Ron Hubbard, "has accomplished the goal of religion expressed in all man's written history, the freeing of the soul by wisdom." With the announcement of that fact, and the proof of workability, a worldwide religion came of age.

Once again, the photographs actually tell us much. "Dianetics and Scientology are coming to the British Isles to stay," he wrote from Phoenix in early 1952, and was soon posing for snapshots in a typically fog-bound London where he lectured at the first British Scientology center. "I am going over to the continent of Europe," he announced, and was next photographed in the Spanish port of Sitges after a whirlwind tour of France, Belgium, Germany and Spain. Then came yet more photographs at his temporary London town house in St. John's Wood, before an Atlantic crossing aboard the *Queen Elizabeth* for yet more lectures at Washington, DC's Shoreham Hotel.

Those lectures, incidentally, were initially of two kinds. First, there was the Scientology congress for the general audience, and generally running two to three days in the larger halls—the aforementioned Shoreham Hotel, for example. With the close of the congress, came the Advanced Clinical Course where new techniques of application were introduced to a smaller audience of professional Scientologists. After 1955, and the establishment of the Founding Church of Scientology in Washington, DC, there were additionally, of course, LRH lectures at the first Scientology Academy and less formal talks before Founding Church staff. But in either case, photographs from these years tend to chronicle a progressive and global growth of Scientology as Ron progressively established Scientology organizations in one city after another. Hence, also, the very telling photographs of Ron in an administrative capacity as Executive Director in Phoenix and latterly at the Founding Church in Washington.

Not necessarily evident, but altogether to the germane, is what Scientology meant to those who appear so inconspicuously here: the attendees of those congresses, students at those Advanced Clinical Courses, parishioners at Phoenix, London and Washington, DC. The point: there are actually people in photographs here who had previously appeared only in wheelchairs owing to an early 1950s polio epidemic. Similarly, there are those who had previously appeared only with crimped limbs and crutches, or may not have appeared at all owing to one or another supposedly incurable illness. Then, of course, are all those who had previously no conception of the happiness, the love, the strength and kindness with which they were capable . . . All of which explains why photographs of Ron from these years were regarded as so precious.

"We have the answers to human suffering and they are available to everyone." – L. Ron Hubbard

Phoenix, Arizona; 1952:
Attendees at the first Scientology lecture series.

Phoenix, Arizona; 1952:
Shortly after the establishment of the first Scientology organization.

*Phoenix, Arizona; 1952:
Ron at the first Scientology
organization. This was the first
Dianetics/Scientology
organization to be directed by
Ron personally. All earlier ones
had been managed by others.*

Camden, New Jersey; 1953:
LRH at the second Hubbard Association
of Scientologists organization.

An early Phoenix lecture with two
microphones for the recording of
Ron's voice and two more for
auditing demonstrations to follow
his opening remarks.

London; circa 1953:
163 Holland Park Avenue, where Ron established the first
British Scientology organization.

*Ron with Founding Scientologist,
George Wichelow and his mobile
Scientology bookstore.*

*Ron with the Triumph
motorcycle for fast excursions
on his 1953 continental tour.*

Phoenix, Arizona; 1954:
Addressing students at one of the more than 450 LRH
lectures delivered that year.

Washington, DC: The LRH office at the new home of the Founding Church on 19th Street NW.

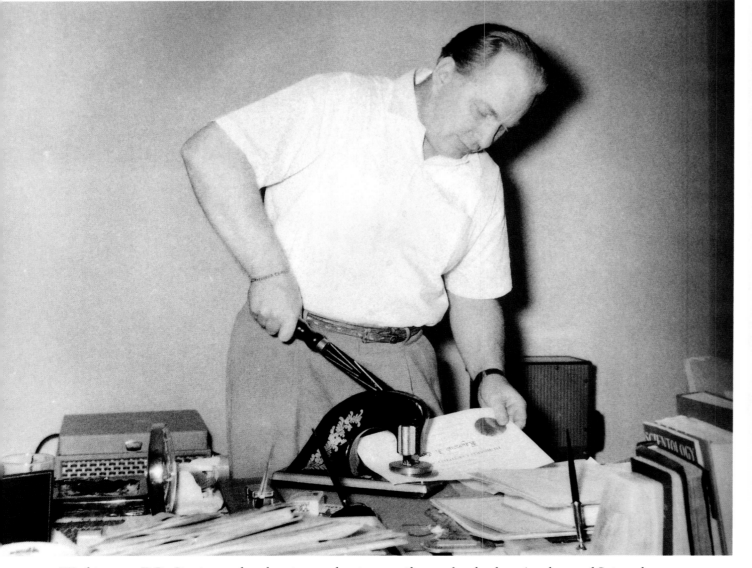

Washington, DC: Signing and embossing graduation certificates for the first Academy of Scientology.

Another view of Ron in his office. The globe, at far left, was presented to Ron by the DC staff and to this day sits in his office in the organization.

Outside his 19th Street, Washington, DC office.

Shoreham Hotel, Washington, DC:
"Here on earth there is an opportunity to construct a civilization such as earth has not before enjoyed." – L. Ron Hubbard

London; 1955:
LRH office at the Hubbard Association of Scientologists International (HASI), at 37 Fitzroy Street.

From the upper floors of this building at 37 Fitzroy Street, Scientology came of age in the United Kingdom.

An early organizational board for British Scientology.

At the Congress on Nuclear Radiation and Health held at the Hall of Nations, Ron released his discoveries relating to the prevention of nuclear conflict and the solution to radioactive proliferation. These discoveries formed the basis of the LRH text known today as All About Radiation.

Mid-Atlantic; 1956:
Returning to Washington aboard the Queen Elizabeth. It was through the course of this voyage that Ron completed a new book on the application of Scientology in the workplace—Problems of Work.

Aboard the Queen Elizabeth; *five-star dining facility (above) and stateroom (below).*

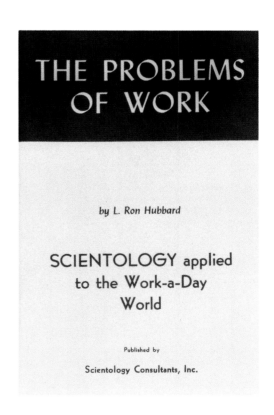

THE PROBLEMS OF WORK

by L. Ron Hubbard

SCIENTOLOGY applied to the Work-a-Day World

Published by

Scientology Consultants, Inc.

Ron and students at the 18th American Advanced Clinical Course where the codified basics of Scientology auditing were repetitively drilled to perfection.

Virginia; 1957:
The Husky *moored near the mouth of the Potomac.*

Anacostia Yacht Harbor, Washington, DC; 1957: Ron eventually kept two vessels moored at Anacostia, for excursions between lecturing and instructing. Pictured is the Chris-Craft, Husky, *with which he regularly plied the Potomac River.*

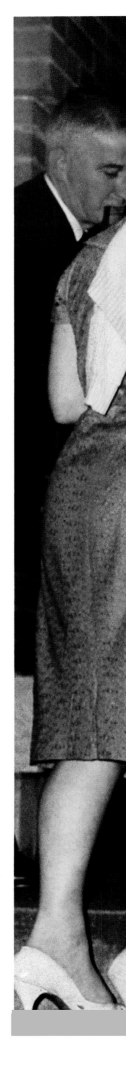

Washington, DC; 1957:
Scientology wedding ceremony in the Founding Church chapel.

"The combined truths of fifty thousand years of thinking men, distilled and amplified by new discoveries about man, have made for this success." – L. Ron Hubbard

"The history of organizations in Dianetics and Scientology is a history of people. It is the history of a number of people finding their feet, finding their initiative and finding their way of life."

L. Ron Hubbard

Shoreham Hotel, Washington, DC; January 1960: State of Man Congress.

SAINT HILL

With the continued growth of Scientology through the latter 1950s, and the consequent need for a truly international training and administrative center, Ron purchased the southern English country estate of Saint Hill. Built from locally quarried sandstone in 1792, and reputedly designed by White House architect Benjamin Henry Latrobe, it stood on fifty-five acres of semi-wooded land in East Grinstead, Sussex. Ron arrived in April 1959, an uncommonly warm April that had left the lawns quite out of hand and the ponds quite choked with weeds. Although mullioned windows admitted only indifferent light, the view across the southern downs was magnificent, with deciduous trees in planned contrast to the evergreens and a Cedar of Lebanon said to be the finest in all England. Thus, Ron's telling note from his first days at Saint Hill: "It's so calm you could pack boxes of serenity out of it. Saint Hill is an exciting place, its terraces banked with flowers, its days crammed with new things."

Local interest was immediate and keen. After all, recalled a reporter attached to Brighton's *Evening Argus*, here was "a genuinely larger than life American author suddenly appearing in our sleepy English midst." Hence, the parade of newspaper reporters traipsing through the still bare halls while Ron congenially explained, the place simply "eats furniture." Meanwhile, these first weeks of April additionally saw his overseeing of physical renovations—repair of the central heating system, the dredging of those weed-choked ponds and restoring the faintly Romanesque swimming pool where he occasionally entertained with extemporized songs on guitar.

Yet when we generally think of Ron's stay at Saint Hill, we tend to think of the technical and administrative breakthroughs that so distinguished these years. For example, it was here he first unveiled the Scientology Organizing Board, delineating the natural pattern for all successful group activities and thus, of course, the pattern of organization for the whole of Scientology. It was also here he inaugurated the Saint Hill Special Briefing Course, and thus the route for a full understanding of Scientology— its theory, application and history of development. Then, too, it was through his six years at Saint Hill Manor that he effectively mapped the heart of Scientology with the Classification and Gradation Chart to delineate each precise step of spiritual advancement through Scientology auditing and training.

The photographs would seem to say it all: The quiet Manor lanes where Ron often strolled the afternoons; LRH seated at his now famous desk, (distinctively draped with a Navajo blanket carried all the way from Phoenix); the rapidly increasing number of Saint Hill staff (finally to total more than two hundred) and the many more hundreds of students who would always recall this place as the home of L. Ron Hubbard.

The world renowned American author at home on the steps of Saint Hill Manor.

167

Saint Hill Manor: "It's a lovely day out and spring bloom is literally covering all our acres." Photograph by L. Ron Hubbard.

Ron generally walked these grounds each afternoon to oversee renovations through the summer of 1959.

As head of the East Grinstead Road Safety Committee Ron also served as the town's Parade Marshal astride his BSA motorcycle.

Ron's flawless Jaguar that made a laughingstock of local speed limits.

"WORKS OF ART
ARE VIEWED BY PEOPLE. THEY
ARE HEARD BY PEOPLE. THEY ARE
FELT BY PEOPLE. THEY ARE
NOT JUST THE FODDER OF
A CLOSE-KNIT GROUP OF
INITIATES. THEY ARE THE SOUL
FOOD OF ALL PEOPLE."

L. RON HUBBARD

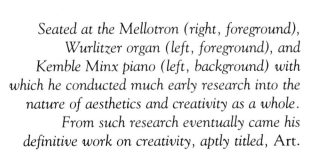

*Seated at the Mellotron (right, foreground),
Wurlitzer organ (left, foreground), and
Kemble Minx piano (left, background) with
which he conducted much early research into the
nature of aesthetics and creativity as a whole.
From such research eventually came his
definitive work on creativity, aptly titled, Art.*

On any typical day, Ron could be found at his desk until the very early hours of the morning.

Three views of the famous LRH office at Saint Hill.
The tiles shown above are a legacy of the Manor's
previous master, the Maharajah of Jaipur.

The filming of LRH lectures.

One of the 437 lectures to students of the Saint Hill Special Briefing Course.

"STANDING OUT ON
A LAWN NEAR A 250-YEAR-OLD
TOWERING CEDAR TREE OR
WALKING THROUGH A PLEASURE
GARDEN, IT'S SO CALM YOU COULD
PACK BOXES OF SERENITY OUT OF IT.
SAINT HILL IS AN EXCITING PLACE,
ITS TERRACES BANKED WITH
FLOWERS, ITS DAYS CRAMMED
WITH NEW THINGS."

L. RON HUBBARD

The famed Rose Garden, Saint Hill Manor.

HORTICULTURAL DISCOVERIES

The fact is, if L. Ron Hubbard had accomplished nothing else through the course of his extraordinary life, he would still be remembered for his 1959/1960 horticultural experimentation at Saint Hill. He initially defined his aims as twofold: First, he wished to examine methods of increasing plant production as a means of reforming world food supplies; while simultaneously—and this is key—he proposed that with the examination of plant life cycles, one might glean pertinent facts regarding the life cycles of all living things. To these aims, he further spoke of radiating seedlings to effect controlled mutations, and eradicating mildew with infrared light.

Results, as evident from the literal fruit of his labor in two Saint Hill greenhouses, were nothing if not dramatic. "His tomatoes keep on growing—to sixteen feet!" exclaimed newspapers of the day, and offered photographs of tomato hybrids producing five times the normal yield, with fifteen trusses and forty-five tomatoes to each. Meanwhile, gardening periodicals marveled at discoveries relating to the restorative properties of infrared baths (spectacularly demonstrated with the rejuvenation of an all but dead orchid). Also of keen interest were LRH sowing techniques for increased germination, and an improved humus composition—all factors for his growing of the earliest sweet corn crop ever seen in England.

From the grander perspective, however, this Saint Hill experimentation concerned much more than plants. Rather, as Ron explained, his work involved a study of life force in general and "cellular life behavior and reaction to see if it was a different *type* of life—it isn't." Ensuing from that research came his delineation of key natural laws relating to *change* as the primary factor in the bettering or worsening of *all* living things.

But however one views Ron's horticultural work from these years, the ramifications were immense. Indeed, if popular conceptions of the plant as a living, feeling organism are now fairly broad, L. Ron Hubbard was actually the first to demonstrate that fact, and his subsequent experimentation proved nothing short of revolutionary.

L. Ron Hubbard as the world of horticulture came to know him through hundreds of newspaper and magazine articles.

"Nearly five hundred cucumbers have been grown two seasons early under experimental conditions at Saint Hill Manor, East Grinstead."
– Evening Standard, *March 21, 1960*

Orchid brought back to life by Mr. Hubbard

Above you see Mr. L. Ron Hubbard – American scientist who now carries out research at East Grinstead, Sussex – holding what is, in fact, a diseased, near-dead orchid. This was taken some months ago. On the left, you see that orchid as it is today – potted and sprouting two new shoots. It's all done by means of light treatment.

This sort of thing – and other interesting experiments in greenhouse automation which Mr. Hubbard is carrying out – form the subject of this week's centre page story and pictures.

8   GARDEN NEWS, Friday, August 21, 1959

He's the 1984 gardener we promised to tell you about

THE DOCTOR SHEDS NEW LIGHT ON MILDEW CURE

ARE you plagued with mildew that attacks growing plants under glass?
Do you know what causes it?
Do you know how to prevent it?

Thanks to the dramatic discoveries of nuclear scientist Dr. Ron Hubbard, we can tell you his answers.

THE CAUSE of mildew in greenhouses? None other than the widely recommended use of bottom heat by either electrical or waterpipe systems.

"In twenty years experimenting I have proved that bottom heat is actually harmful," Dr. Hubbard says. "It is the probable cause of all damp diseases and fungus that attacks so many greenhouses in winter."

THE CURE for mildew is simple and inexpensive. The doctor's prescription: install an infrared ray lamp in your glasshouse like a normal light. "By this method I've discovered how to completely check and prevent the spread of mildew," he proclaims.

This is no idle theorising on Dr. Hubbard's part. At Saint Hill Manor estate, near East Grinstead in Sussex, we saw enough evidence of his researches to support his assertion that current experiments he is conducting are 25 years in advance of today's methods and ideas.

In his laboratories Dr. Hubbard has developed some brand-new ideas based on the relationship of artificial light to plant growth. One experiment, results of which you see in the photograph on the right, involved the growing of tomato plants under different coloured lights. **The results were startling.**

One interesting point about this particular test of reactions to colours was that under a green light the soil dried out very quickly.

The doctor's explanation is this: "It seems that a green light has some molecular reaction on the water which dries it much quicker than other lights. This could

have its own individual application–drying out a house, to give just one example."

What else has been done at Saint Hill Manor?

Recently in *Garden News* Dr. Hubbard claimed he could produce a tomato plant with five times the normal fruit-bearing capacity. **THIS HE HAS DONE.**

EVER-BEARING

Grown from seeds treated by radiation, plants are growing like vines, are apparently ever-bearing, and each contains 15 trusses with no less than 45 fruits on each truss.

"Seeds from these plants had grown in the same way without any additional treatment by radiation," the scientist told us.

There in the glasshouses, too, is sweet corn that has already grown to 12 feet instead of the usual five feet. The output of corn by each plant is estimated to be five times greater than if grown under normal field conditions.

"At Saint Hill Manor estate, near East Grinstead in Sussex, we saw enough evidence of Mr. Hubbard's researches to support assertion that current experiments are twenty-five years in advance of today's methods and ideas . . ."
– Garden News, *August 21, 1959*

"We want to find what constitutes the perfect growing soil which will take a plant to maturity—not just a rooting or potting medium."
– L. Ron Hubbard

"Thus it is clear," reported the Garden News of October 2, 1959 on Ron's light tests, *"that geraniums have responded best to ordinary tungsten and infrared lights, these plants being up to a third bigger than the others and flowering well."*

"On and on they grow." – Toronto Daily Star, July 5, 1960

"I FOUND THAT WE MUST
HAVE A BETTER COMMUNICATION WITH
PLANTS, IF WE ARE EVER TO BEGIN TO
UNDERSTAND THEM AND USE THEM TO
THE FULLEST ADVANTAGE OF MANKIND."

L. RON HUBBARD

LRH's Saint Hill horticultural experiments involved a study of life force in general and as he explained, "cellular life behavior and reaction to see if it was a different type of life—it isn't."

SOUTH TO AFRICA

Although Ron had long kept an eye on a burgeoning Scientology in South Africa, it was not until spring 1960, that he made his first journey to the continent. The catalyst was a report from South African friend and Scientologist Peggy Conway, regarding the alleged per capita insanity rates among Blacks and their eventual treatment at the hands of psychiatrists. As an initial observation, Ron wrote: "My records show (and will have to do until I can make a closer survey myself) that the number of insane and neurotic persons runs much higher than amongst comparable populations." He further expressed his concern regarding the larger sociopolitical fate of these people . . . which was to say, the native African is "already overwhelmed by bad food and disease without adding insanity amongst its familial units."

He arrived in April, to take a house on the Linksfield Ridge. Initial days were spent lecturing at a then newly established Scientology center in Joubert Park, while evenings were very significantly devoted to broader national concerns.

What was finally to come from these evenings was a then fairly remarkable document: an LRH constitution calling for universal African suffrage. His point, and even conservative circles could hardly dispute it: if South Africa was to enjoy foreign investment, she must end her repression of the Black.

His recommended constitution for the then southern African nation of Rhodesia (where he landed in March 1966 to establish a Scientology center and research base near Salisbury) contained the same argument. Quite apart from inherent inequity of apartheid, he maintained, no nation can hope for a stable economic/political climate when the majority of citizens are not afforded fundamental human rights. Hence, his repeated appeal for what he described as "One Man—One Vote," regardless of race, color or creed.

Inevitably, of course, Ron's stance on what ruling Whites termed the "native question" led to considerable trouble. To wit: Ron was to be effectively barred from Rhodesia as a willful threat to white supremacy. And, in fact, the charge was valid. What he stood for and what he fought for was, indeed, nothing less than political and spiritual freedom of all African people . . . Which, incidentally, accounts for why he was so thoroughly gratified when, a decade later, his educational tools were introduced into native schools for the benefit of some two million Black African children.

Images presented here, however, record his fight, not his ultimate victory. Among other notes of interest regarding photographs through the pages to follow: members of his Rhodesian household staff affectionately called him "Rhino," because he was strong and unwavering, and because of the way in which he charged through the bush in an old Land Rover. When members of that same staff first examined Ron's household organizing board (adopted from the Scientology organizing board) they were said to have grown "at least two feet right on the spot." For no longer were they "servants," but were instead domestic professionals with honorable duties and authority. Lastly, and although not necessarily visible in the photographs, when he finally bid farewell to those people, their faces were tracked with tears.

Southern Africa; 1966:
Where, as Ron modestly put it, "Adventures were many."

Johannesburg, South Africa; 1961: Black South African women.
Photograph by L. Ron Hubbard.

At a South African township for talks with Black leaders, and a tribal celebration.
Photographs by L. Ron Hubbard.

Overlooking an African township where Ron's educational tools would eventually mean so much.

"YOU KNOW, I'M VERY FOND OF
JOBURG. I HAVE WALKED UP YOUR HILLS AND MY LIPS HAVE TURNED
BLUE AND I HAVE PUFFED FROM THE RAREFIED AIR. I WATCHED
THIS RAIN COME DOWN FROM THE SKY, HIT THE GROUND AND
BOUNCE UP AGAIN ABOUT THREE FEET AND FILL MY BOOTS. I HAVE
ENJOYED YOUR PLEASANT SKIES AND AS A MATTER OF FACT, I HAVE
MYSELF QUITE A LONG HISTORY IN SOUTHERN AFRICA."

L. RON HUBBARD

Johannesburg, South Africa; 1961:
With the Minister of Black South
African Affairs.

The Constitution, Bill of Rights and Penal Code LRH proffered to the nations of South Africa and Rhodesia in the name of equality, stability and fundamental human rights.

Representing the Black South African cause (above and below) with South African ministers.

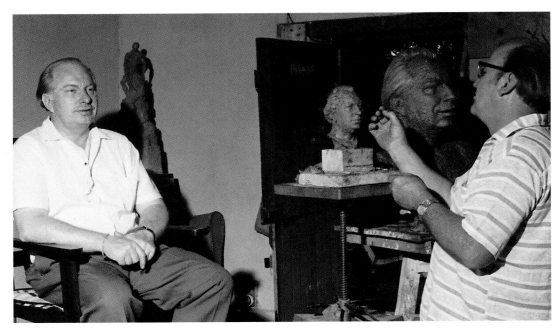

Johannesburg; 1961: The smaller-scale bust.

Johannesburg; 1961: World renowned South African sculptor, Cooert Steynberg fashions the bust of LRH now found in virtually every Scientology organization worldwide.

Johannesburg; 1961: Mr. Steynberg presents LRH and South African Scientologists with his sculpture of the Founder.

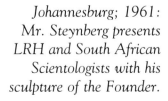

Salisbury, Rhodesia; 1966:
With his Rhodesian staff.

L. Ron Hubbard's Salisbury home.

Lake Kariba in Rhodesia where Ron worked to improve employment conditions for all natives.

Salisbury; July 1966:
"I pray to God with tears in my eyes that you will come back into this country and emancipate us. Everyone who worked for you is wishing you the best of everything, and hope you won't forget Africa and its troubles." – Frank Masiko, LRH Chauffeur

"THIS WORK
DOES NOT REPRESENT A
REVOLT; IT DOESN'T EVEN
VAGUELY REPRESENT A DESIRE
FOR THE DEMISE OF ANY OF
THESE THINGS. ALL IT
REPRESENTS IS THE HOPE
THAT MAN AGAIN CAN FIND
HIS OWN FEET."

L. RON HUBBARD

PHOTOGRAPHER

As suggested by so many images here, L. Ron Hubbard had long loved the art of "writing with light," as he termed it. A keen student of photography through his youth, his professional career effectively began in the 1920s with the sale of his first Asian studies (including his Great Wall of China presented earlier) to *National Geographic*. As a student at George Washington University, he continued to work in a professional capacity as both a photojournalist for the *Washington Herald* and on a freelance basis for national magazines. Of particular note were his aerial photographs (also presented earlier) for the *Sportsman Pilot*.

With his residence at Saint Hill Manor through the early 1960s, his photographic output dramatically increased with award-winning landscapes, pastorals, action and still life—several of which were eventually selected for exhibition at the International Photography Exhibition in Nantes, France and the Versailles Salon International d'Art Photographique. The Saint Hill years may also be remembered for his reexamination of photographic fundamentals with the New York Institute of Photography, and his experimentation with then cutting-edge techniques and equipment. (He was, for example, in correspondence with Professor Land of Polaroid regarding refinement of the Land camera.)

The succeeding decade saw him behind the camera for various government agencies and national tourist boards throughout Europe and the Caribbean, notably represented here in sequences from Spain and Portugal. Additionally from the 1970s, came his benchmark procedures for the testing of film and equipment, his advancement of thirty-five-millimeter techniques, his redefinition of photographic composition and his several hundred instructional essays—all for the final delineation of how we best write with light.

With his long-favored Rolleiflex in the pastures beyond Saint Hill Manor; 1965.

On the grounds of Saint Hill with a large format Linhof used for portraits and scenics.

The Linhof (right) and the Voigtlander (below) for the early testing of then novel projected images for use as studio backgrounds.

The Linhof for an indoor self-portrait against the projected background.

"LIFE IS LIGHT.
YOU CAN MAKE LIGHT DO ANYTHING YOU
WANT TO. PHOTOGRAPHY MEANS
'LIGHT WRITING.'"

L. RON HUBBARD

Multiple exposure, 1965.
Photograph by L. Ron Hubbard.

Saint Hill; 1965:
Self-portrait in an oval mirror.

With a Voigtlander (one of the first thirty-five-millimeter cameras) at an East Grinstead riding academy. At his side is a "Rollei."

With Rolleiflex capturing an equestrian event.

The terrace steps of Saint Hill with one of his several Rolleis, for study of the Rose Garden.

Grand Canary; 1965:
With Graflex on a photographic tour of the Canaries conducted partly on behalf of the Spanish tourist board.

Agadir, Morocco; 1971: Photograph by L. Ron Hubbard.

Oporto, Portugal; 1972:
Photograph by L. Ron Hubbard.

Oporto, Portugal; 1972:
A photographic essay of Oporto wineries on
behalf of the local trade association.

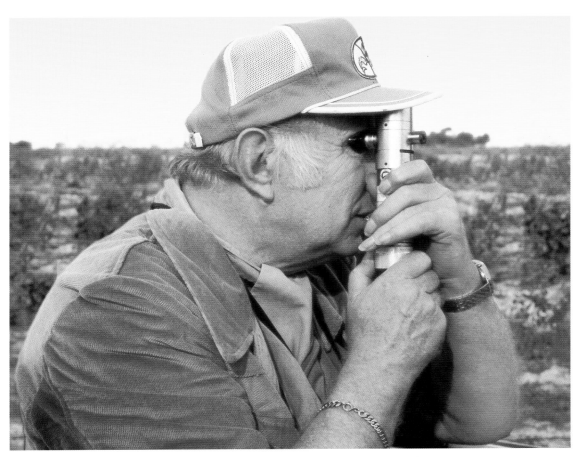

Taking a reading with a light meter for shots of the Oporto vineyards.

"ARTISTIC PRESENTATION
ALWAYS SUCCEEDS TO THE DEGREE THAT IT IS DONE *WELL*.
HOW *EASILY* IT IS DONE IS ENTIRELY SECONDARY."

L. RON HUBBARD

Photo shoot with his Pentax in Oporto, Portugal; 1972.

Cadiz, Spain; 1974:
Festival of Lights.

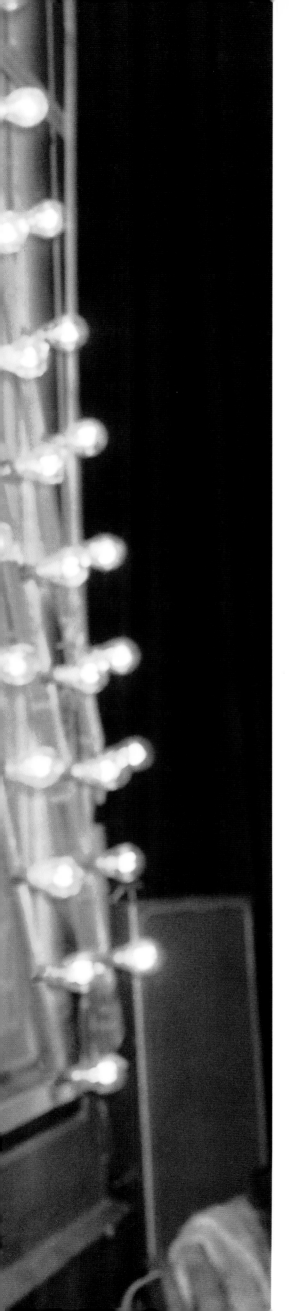

"In any artistic
production, what does one have as an audience?
People. Not, heaven forbid, critics. But people.
Not experts in that line of art. But people."

L. Ron Hubbard

RETURN TO THE SEA

With the intensity of research beyond September of 1966, particularly as regards the highest levels of the Scientology Bridge, Ron left his home at Saint Hill Manor and returned to the sea. In simple explanation, he spoke of a need to remove himself from administrative concerns and establish a facility off the busy "crossroads of the world." Simultaneously, however, he also now spoke of a need to guarantee the future of Scientology in a precarious world, to preserve its materials and provide for safe passage through those extraordinary upper levels. What ensued was, of course, the Sea Organization—that supremely dedicated body formed to both assist Ron with research and safeguard the Scientology Bridge. What also, of course, ensued were the first vessels of that organization, including *Enchanter* (later rechristened *Diana*), and a stout North Sea trawler, *Avon River*. Then naturally followed Ron's assumption of duties as Commodore, and his billing and drilling of the first crews for what he described as a comfortable relationship with "Old Man Sea." Finally, in late 1967, came acquisition of the third and largest Sea Organization vessel—the 3,200 ton *Royal Scotman,* later rechristened *Apollo*—serving as Ron's home and Flagship for the next eight years.

Needless to say adventures from these years were many: the skirting of a hurricane off the Azores, a brush with real pirates off Sardinia and a legendary archaeological expedition known as Mission into Time. Then, too, and rather more to the point, came all that these years represented for Scientology, including the Sea Organization's assumption of worldwide managerial duties, the commensurate growth of both the Sea Organization itself and the religion as a whole, and Ron's ceaseless advancement of his spiritual technology into higher and higher realms.

With continued Sea Organization growth through the early 1970s, and their expansion efforts for the whole of Scientology, Ron and crew finally stepped back ashore to establish the Flag Land Base at Clearwater, Florida. Then followed his move to the southern California desert community at La Quinta where he saw to the forming of a cinematic unit for the production of Scientology training films.

In either case, however, these images from the sea will stand forever—in no small part for the fact that Ron both encouraged the photographic work of others and was himself often seen with a camera. As noted, he had often carried his equipment in a wholly professional capacity—on behalf of trade/tourist agencies in various Atlantic and Caribbean ports of call. (Portuguese President Marcelo Caetano, for example, sat for Ron's camera.) Just as frequently, however, he shot for the sheer love of shooting, and thereby captured what is otherwise difficult to convey: "The joy I take in the singing wind and sea." Then again, we are also left with the very telling photographs of the man to convey what is equally ineffable: Here is the Commodore at home on his vessel.

The Commodore, 1969.

Tenerife, Canary Islands; circa 1969: The double-ended high-sided ketch, Enchanter *that served as Ron's original research vessel.*

"I was using a small yacht—the Enchanter—and although she is a steel vessel and very, very strong, she nevertheless was operating in seas which were far beyond her class and capability."
– L. Ron Hubbard

"To learn to be a sailor is simply to learn to predict what trouble you're not going to get into." – L. Ron Hubbard

Aboard the Enchanter *in the Canary Islands; 1967.*

"WHEN YOU REALIZE THAT THE OLD-TIMERS DID THEIR GREAT VOYAGES OF DISCOVERY IN SHIPS VERY LITTLE BIGGER THAN *ENCHANTER*, YOU WILL SEE THEY HAD THEIR NERVE WITH THEM."

L. RON HUBBARD

The Avon River *and the* Enchanter.

Towers at Castellammare del Golfo, Sicily; 1967:
Before arriving in Sicilian waters, Ron had sketched a map from past life memory, to indicate the presence of cellars beneath these towers. Upon investigation, the expedition party found precisely what Ron had predicted.

"Just recently," announced the Explorers Club in 1967, "Mr. Hubbard was again awarded custody of the Explorers Club flag for the Hubbard Geological Survey Expedition. The purpose of this expedition is to find and examine relics and artifacts and so amplify man's knowledge of history." Also known as Mission into Time, the expedition further provided for the testing of past life recall. That is, without reference to any material guide, Sea Organization teams were able to pinpoint archaeological sites with Ron's sketches drawn from whole track experience along these very same coasts.

Ron off Grand Canary during Mission into Time.

Italian waters; 1967.

"THE SHIP IS AN
UNREAL, FRAGILE THING, FULL OF STRANGE
GROANS, AND ENGINE AND SAILS ARE
DWARFED IN THEIR PUNY POWER WHEN
MATCHED TO ALL THE COUNTLESS
HORSEPOWER IN WAVE AND WIND AND
CURRENT."

L. RON HUBBARD

The christening of the Apollo, Corfu; November 1968:
"You have a whole world to sail in and we thank you very much for
staying afloat and serving us so well and long may you survive."
– L. Ron Hubbard

Taking a bearing.

Off the coast of Morocco; 1972:
On the flying bridge. Beside him stands the Magnetic Standard Compass, against
which other Apollo compasses were calibrated.

The Flagship Apollo *in Curaçao after her Atlantic crossing in 1974. Photograph by L. Ron Hubbard.*

1968: Drilling his crew aboard the Apollo.

"A sailor has to put something under him. The nearest ground is often thousands of feet down. And he has to put something around him that can stand up to the elements or get the full force of high winds and waves."
– L. Ron Hubbard

1969: Shortly after refit where the Apollo's stack received its distinctive "LRH."

At his desk in the research room drafting yet another instructional memo on shipboard procedures.

On the promenade deck where he often took short breaks during long nights of research.

At the staff bulletin board where notices regarding both shipboard life and international news were posted.

Aboard the Apollo; *1972.*

"THERE HAS BEEN JOY AND
LAUGHTER AND HIGH ADVENTURE
BUT IT ALWAYS HAD A PURPOSE."

L. RON HUBBARD

"It is the Master's task to bring about an atmosphere of confidence through the exhibition of personal competence."

L. Ron Hubbard

At the helm.

At the chart table.

On the bridge.

Descending to the aft deck to brief the crew. Tape recordings of LRH briefings and lectures through this period constitute part of the training materials for every Sea Organization member today.

"Old Man Sea is the most amenable old fellow you ever met in your life—he hasn't got a kind bone in his body but he does respect a ship which is well drilled." – L. Ron Hubbard

At sea aboard the Apollo; 1972:
A model of the Cutty Sark on the mantel of
Ron's research room, painstakingly built by
members of the crew as a gift to their
Commodore.

Off the coast of Tunisia; 1968:
Ron aboard his Chris-Craft.

"GOOD LUCK,
CALM SEAS, GOOD FRIENDS
AND BON VOYAGE TO
ALL OF YOU."

L. RON HUBBARD

IMAGES IN PORTRAIT

A s Ron himself once remarked, the way in which we conceive of him from his work and the application of his technology, is, in fact, the truth. Our sense of the man as supremely caring, supremely compassionate, supremely dedicated and wise—all this is the truth.

Reflective of that fact is the affection he inspires in so many millions worldwide. (Each March 13th, for example, draws more people together in active celebration than the birthday of any twentieth-century figure.)

Yet just as reflective of the essential L. Ron Hubbard, the L. Ron Hubbard conceived of in the hearts of those who know him through his work, is the series of portraits presented here. They are offered with no other commentary than selections from his own writings, and otherwise tell us exactly who he is.

"FROM THE AGE OF THREE
I KNEW EXACTLY WHERE I WAS GOING. THIS HAS
BEEN A LIFE OF STEADY DEDICATION AND FORWARD
PROGRESS."

L. RON HUBBARD

"I HAVE SEEN LIFE
FROM THE TOP DOWN AND THE
BOTTOM UP. I KNOW HOW IT LOOKS
BOTH WAYS. AND I KNOW THERE *IS*
WISDOM AND THAT THERE IS HOPE."

L. RON HUBBARD

"MY PURPOSE IS TO BRING
A BARBARISM OUT OF THE MUD IT THINKS CONCEIVED
IT AND TO FORM, HERE ON EARTH, A CIVILIZATION
BASED ON HUMAN UNDERSTANDING."

L. RON HUBBARD

"Wisdom is meant for anyone who wishes to reach for it. It is the servant of the commoner and king alike and should never be regarded with awe."

L. RON HUBBARD

"I LIKE TO HELP OTHERS AND
COUNT IT AS MY GREATEST PLEASURE IN LIFE TO SEE A PERSON
FREE HIMSELF OF THE SHADOWS WHICH DARKEN HIS DAYS. THESE
SHADOWS LOOK SO THICK TO HIM AND WEIGH HIM DOWN SO
THAT WHEN HE FINDS THEY *ARE* SHADOWS AND THAT HE CAN SEE
THROUGH THEM, WALK THROUGH THEM AND BE AGAIN IN THE SUN,
HE IS ENORMOUSLY DELIGHTED. AND I AM AFRAID I AM JUST
AS DELIGHTED AS HE IS."

L. RON HUBBARD

IN SUMMARY
OF A LIFETIME

Obviously no series of photographs, however extensive, can possibly convey what L. Ron Hubbard finally represents to those who have benefited from the fact that he lived. Rather, we have seen but the images leading to his life's work—the far-flung journeys of discovery, the tireless years of research, the literature with which he supported that research, the founding and development of a religious philosophy towards:

"A civilization without insanity, without criminals and without war, where the able can prosper and honest beings can have rights, and where man is free to rise to greater heights."

Yet in summation, let us at least glance at what lies behind the photographs here, these images from L. Ron Hubbard's remarkable lifetime . . .

The materials of Dianetics and Scientology are contained in some five thousand writings and three thousand tape-recorded lectures. The essential truths within those materials are now embraced by millions on all continents and from all lands where Ron walked—Blackfeet in Montana, tribal communities in Africa, residents on those South Pacific isles and right across the face of Asia to the Western hills of China. Moreover, their numbers grow by some ten thousand every week, so that in addition to the several thousand organizations currently offering LRH technologies, another hundred such organizations open their doors each year.

What draws those millions to Ron's work and, in turn, is drawn from the greater body of truths within Dianetics and Scientology, are the LRH solutions to what most plagues this civilization. For example, among other discoveries from his stay at Saint Hill came answers to what has undermined twentieth-century education. In consequence, some three million students, many of whom were once wholly illiterate, now read and write with Ron's educational tools. Among other developments from his years as Executive Director of Scientology internationally, came LRH administrative tools for sane and equitable management. In consequence, employees of thirty-five thousand companies and corporations in forty nations are now prospering with LRH Administrative Technology. From research aboard the *Apollo* in the early 1970s, and subsequent work through the remainder of that decade, came an LRH program for drug rehabilitation that is rightfully deemed the world's most successful and has thus far returned some hundred thousand former addicts to a drug-free life. From research in Los Angeles through the late 1940s, came the LRH program for criminal reform, also known to be the singularly most successful, and so utilized in penal institutions across six continents. Finally, and in addition to all else through the early 1980s, came his nonreligious moral code, *The Way to Happiness*, now in the hands of at least fifty million people to help rebuild the moral fabric in communities across every landscape seen in photographs here.

So no, the real culmination of images here cannot be represented in a photograph. After all, how can the camera possibly capture what L. Ron Hubbard means to a former drug addict in Washington, DC, a former illiterate in Los Angeles, a previously impoverished shopkeeper in southern Africa, or a once crime-ravaged neighborhood in New York City? Then, too, how can the camera possibly capture what he means to all those many millions more who have found a spiritual fulfillment in Dianetics and Scientology that cannot even be described with words?

The sixty-three million words of L. Ron Hubbard that have so deeply touched readers in virtually every nation on earth. Each individual title in this photograph is a separate LRH work including more than three thousand lectures, eighty-four films, three encyclopedic series and more than five hundred novels and collections of short stories.